DATE DUE

THE DECISIVE HOUR OF
CHRISTIAN MISSIONS

WORLD MISSIONARY CONFERENCE, UNITED FREE CHURCH ASSEMBLY HALL, EDINBURGH

THE DECISIVE HOUR

OF

CHRISTIAN MISSIONS

BY

JOHN R. MOTT

NEW YORK
STUDENT VOLUNTEER MOVEMENT
FOR FOREIGN MISSIONS
1910

266
M85d

PREFACE

THE World Missionary Conference held in Edinburgh in June of the present year constituted in its plan, in its personnel, in the spirit which characterized it, and in its promise, the most significant gathering ever held in the interest of the world's evangelization. In preparation for the Conference eight representative international Commissions had been at work for over eighteen months making a scientific investigation and study of some of the most pressing and vital problems of Christian missions. Associated with these Commissions as correspondents were the principal missionaries and leaders of the Church on the mission fields, as well as many of the foremost thinkers and workers of the missionary forces at home. The reports resulting from these special investigations have afforded a very comprehensive presentation of the facts about the main aspects of the missionary situation. Those who have had opportunity to examine the mass of evidence gathered by the Commissions and to listen to the discussions of the reports at the Edinburgh Conference must have been impressed with the fact that the present is the decisive hour of Christian missions. In the history of Christianity there has never been such a remarkable conjunction of opportunities and crises on all the principal mission fields and of favoring circumstances and possibilities on the home field.

The central idea of this book has been suggested by

172

the studies in connection with Commission I on " Carrying the Gospel to all the Non-Christian World " of which the author was chairman. He has made large use of the results of the investigations of the Commission, and has introduced without quotation certain parts of the report written by himself. He has also profited by the investigations made by the other Commissions and by the debates of the Conference itself. The book is based, therefore, almost entirely upon the information furnished recently by trusted correspondents, representing every part of the world under review, and not, save in rare cases, upon material accessible in print. Reports of the eight Commissions are soon to be printed and readers who wish to follow further the subjects under consideration are referred to these volumes. As they have not yet appeared, the plan of giving references to them in foot-notes has had to be abandoned. Nearly all of the quotations in different chapters are from correspondence preserved in the Archives of the World Missionary Conference.

The author wishes to acknowledge his deep indebtedness to the members and correspondents of Commission I. He has been greatly helped by the generous and efficient co-operation of the Editorial Committee of the United Council for Mission Study of Great Britain, as well as by that of Dr. T. H. P. Sailer, a recognized authority on mission study. He is under particular obligation to Mr. Hans P. Andersen for his wise and constant help.

JOHN R. MOTT

EDINBURGH, June 29, 1910

CONTENTS

LIST OF ILLUSTRATIONS

THE NON-CHRISTIAN NATIONS
PLASTIC AND CHANGING

THE DECISIVE HOUR OF
CHRISTIAN MISSIONS

CHAPTER I

THE NON-CHRISTIAN NATIONS PLASTIC AND CHANGING

THROUGHOUT the non-Christian world there are unmistakable signs of the awakening of great peoples from their long sleep. Through the whole of Asia a ferment is in process, which has spread from the intellectual leaders, and is fast taking possession of the masses. It affects over three-fourths of the human race, including peoples of high intelligence and ancient civilization. The leaders are concerned with the questions of enlightenment, of intellectual and social freedom, of economic development, and of national efficiency. In all history there has not been a period when such vast multitudes of people were in the midst of such stupendous changes, economic, social, educational, and religious. Among innumerable multitudes of the inhabitants of the non-Christian world the forces of youth and age, of radicalism and conservatism, of growth and decay, are seething and struggling for the mastery. As we survey the unparalleled situation in

3

these lands, the question is forced upon us, What is to be the issue of it all?

It is difficult to believe that two generations ago Japan was even more completely closed to Western influence than was China. She was then under a feudal form of government, divided into clans; those of the warrior clan, the Samurai, were intensely devoted to their lords and jealous of the other clans. The rights of the common people were greatly restricted. One policy was rigidly enforced—exclusion of the foreigner and of foreign customs. No Japanese was permitted to leave the country, and any who escaped were not permitted to return. Not until 1868 did a revolution make the Emperor actual as well as nominal head of the nation. In 1871 the feudal lords voluntarily surrendered their rule, and, at the advice of a missionary, an embassy was sent to Western lands to observe and report. This tour led to the systematic appropriation of Western ideas, culminating in a constitutional government proclaimed in 1889. Since then Japan has proved herself, in some respects, the most brilliant nation in the world. She has achieved greater progress in one generation than any other country has achieved in two, if not in three generations. She has gone to school to the whole world and has learned her lessons with remarkable facility. Seldom does the traveler find himself upon an ocean steamer that he does not discover among his fellow-passengers one or more Japanese—not going about the world in search of pleasure, but journeying with serious intent to study some institution, some movement, some process, some experience of another nation or people, determined to make this larger knowledge tributary to the expanding greatness of their own country. Open-mindedness is their characteristic as a people. Some have feared that their recent victories would make them proud, but those who have been in touch with Japan have received an opposite impression. They have found that the Japanese have rather been humbled and solemnized by their victories, and have come to have an increased sense of responsibility. Possibly never has Japan manifested greater eagerness to learn from other nations and to increase her efficiency than during the period which has elapsed since the Russian war. The view entertained in some quarters that Japan has at last become fixed is incorrect. She has not ceased to go to school. Her time of transition has not wholly passed and profound changes are still taking place, if not so rapidly as before.

The fact must not be lost sight of that influences from Japan extend over the whole Orient. The leaders of the Japanese Christian Student Movement emphasized this fact in a cable message which they sent to the Student Volunteer Convention in Nashville, in 1906, "Japan is leading the Orient, but whither?" Even more aptly do these words express the position of Japan to-day than at the time when the message was sent. The most casual traveler sees how Japan is becoming an increasing factor in the commercial and industrial developments of the Far East, and the great steamship agencies of America, Britain, and Germany feel the pressure of this fact increasingly. Japan is profoundly influencing the economic changes, not only of Korea but also of China. Her voice has become the most influential in the political councils of the Far East. To a far greater extent than most people realize she has taken the leading position in the promotion of the educational movement on the mainland of Asia. True it is that Japan is leading the Orient. The Eastern nations are following Japan, as Japan is following the West, and what Japan has succeeded in doing to-day the others will do to-morrow. The advance of Japan is a prophecy of what will follow throughout the nations of the East.

Korea was known yesterday as " The Land of the Morning Calm." Not till 1883 was the first treaty made with a Western nation and the first foreigner permitted to live in the land. Even up to 1907, at which time Japan assumed practically complete control, the Government was most unprogressive. To-day Korea is vibrating with the spirit of the modern world, and the age-long isolation of the hermit nation has ceased. Where are ten millions of people to be found upon whom the currents of modern civilization have been turned more abruptly, and with greater directness and power, than upon the Korean people during the last five years? A railway has been stretched across the whole length of the peninsula. The material resources of the country are being rapidly developed, the Government having within recent years granted nearly two hundred mining concessions. Other new and profitable industries are being introduced. The educational system has been reformed along modern lines, and the people are so fully awake to the value and necessity of Western knowledge and education that they will take whatever literature or teacher will help to meet this demand. A new literature is being evolved under the influence of the Christian Church. A new and highly efficient financial system has been introduced. Countless other economic and political changes have been effected. Far-reaching social changes, such as the raising of the age for marriage and the gradual doing away with the custom of concubinage, are taking place. Torture has been eliminated from the penal code. In fact, every department of the life of the country is being reorganized. Their present political condition, which is very bitter to them, has served to arouse the Koreans from their self-satisfied lethargy. The old ways will no longer do, and they know it. Their eyes have been opened to what the West has to teach them, and they are absorbing new methods with great rapidity.

For four thousand years China has been the same unchanging empire, entirely self-centered and self-satisfied, with a profound contempt for everything foreign. Yet to-day she too has turned her face from the past and begun to learn from other nations. The changeless is giving way to the changing, and the changes are bewildering in their number and variety. She has made a more radical adjustment to modern conditions within the last five years than has any other nation, not excepting Korea. Those who have studied the great changes that came over Japan will remember that she made no such advance in the first ten years after she began to adopt Western civilization as China has made during the last five years. Sir Robert Hart, the eminent civilian and sagacious observer of things Chinese, in commenting on the recent changes in China, said that during the first forty-five years of his residence in China the country was like a closed room, without a breath of fresh air from the outside world, but that the last five years reminded him of being in a room with all the windows and doors wide open and the breezes of heaven sweeping through. Dr. Griffith John, one of China's greatest missionaries, on starting back from his last furlough, in speaking to a group of Christian workers in America, said that if the recent changes which had taken place in China had been attended with the bloodshed which characterized the late Russian revolution, the eyes of the civilized world would be fixed upon China, and nothing would hold back the Christian nations from going to her relief. President Lowry of the Peking University insists that the change which has come over China within the last decade has been so great that it is " almost impossible to describe the contrast with the past without seeming extravagance of language." He regards it as " one of the most sweeping and radical revolutions ever effected in any great nation in the history of the world."

Only twenty years ago the telegraph system of China was confined to a few wires binding together

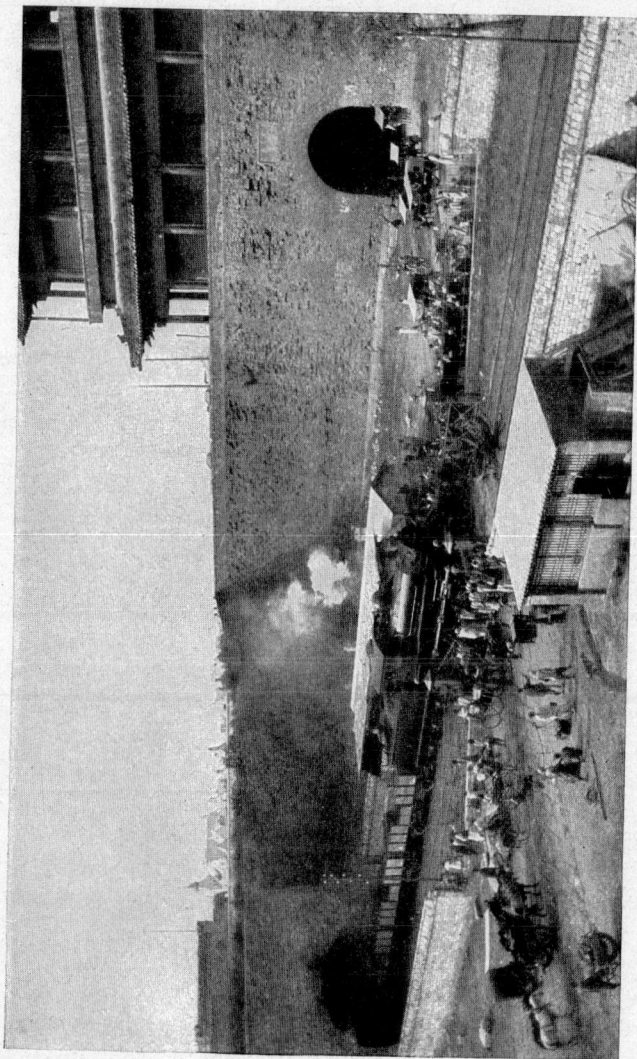

RAILWAY PENETRATING THE OLD WALL OF PEKING

the port cities; now a network of 26,000 miles of telegraph lines, connecting with 490 telegraph offices, is
spread over the empire.   For thousands of years, rivers
and canals were the principal channels of communication in this country, but in recent years the railway has
come in as the great rival.   In 1895 there were but 200
miles of railway in China; now there are 4170 miles in
operation and 9000 miles more projected.*   The
journey can now be made in a *train de luxe* from Peking to Hankow in the heart of China in thirty-six
hours, whereas six years ago it would have required
fully forty days by Chinese carts.   Steamer lines cover
a distance of 8000 miles.   The Yangtse from Hankow
to Shanghai sustains a greater traffic than any other
river in the world for an equal distance.   All the great
port cities of China and some of those along the inland rivers are being rapidly modernized, and remind
one of the crowded commercial ports of the West.
Great modern industrial plants are being rapidly established in and near the large interior cities, as well as at
the ports.   In Hankow alone not less than 25,000 men
are employed in such establishments.   Shanghai, which
a generation ago was comparatively but a river village,
to-day has a tonnage in its harbor next to that of
Liverpool.   Only a few years ago there were no modern post offices; now they are to be found in 3500
towns and cities, and the number is increasing day by
day.   In many cities the rushlight has been superseded
by the electric light.   The fear of " boring into the
pulse of the dragon" is being lost by those who are

* See map at the end of this volume.

anxious to exploit the mineral wealth of the country.

Twelve years ago there was only one daily paper in Peking, the ancient *Peking Gazette,* devoted chiefly to publishing the edicts of the Imperial Government. Now, there are said to be ten dailies there. In the other cities throughout China, hundreds of modern periodicals have been established, all of which devote a large section of their space to reporting news from all parts of the world. The printing-presses, both those under secular, and those under missionary auspices, are not able to keep pace with the demand made upon them for the bringing out of new works and of translations of the books of important authors of Western nations.

Political changes of far-reaching importance have been effected. Constitutional government has recently been promised by Imperial edict. October 14, 1909, will henceforth be a historic date in China, because on that day provincial assemblies were opened in the capitals of all the provinces. This is a significant step in the ten-years' programme which is to culminate in the actual establishment of modern parliamentary constitutional government for the Chinese Empire. The work of these new assemblies during the intervening years is to serve as a means of preparing the people for the new political responsibilities involved. Those who have had opportunity to study these assemblies bear testimony that, even in their first year, in the strength of their personnel, in the wisdom with which they have dealt with the subjects before them, in the dignity with

which the discussions have been conducted, in the order
and practical efficiency with which they carry on
business, these bodies impress them quite as favorably
as do the political assemblies of some of the Western
nations, both in Europe and in North and South
America. Already the work of these assemblies in
some of the provinces has passed beyond the realm of
academic discussion into that of evolving practical
measures concerning both the immediate and the future
welfare of the country. In October of the present year
(1910) the Imperial Senate will hold its first meeting.

Without doubt the best illustration of the social and
moral progress of the New China is the anti-opium
crusade. The Imperial Government in 1907 decided
that the opium evil must be extirpated from China. It
was agreed that this must be accomplished within ten
years. The official regulations, which are understood
to have been prepared by Tang Shao Yi, one of the
Imperial Commissioners on Opium Suppression, are so
masterly in their scope, as well as in their practical
details, that they are worthy of study by the statesmen
and reformers of other lands. The Government prohibited the use of opium by all officials except those of
very advanced age. In a wonderful way persons high
in political and social circles in all parts of China have
thrown themselves into the movement. It is said that
some of the princes and officials have died as a result
of their most zealous and serious struggles to break
the opium habit. All over China popular societies have
been formed for the purpose of waging the anti-opium
propaganda. Great mass-meetings have been held in

the principal cities and in many towns. The assembling and burning of opium-smoking outfits is no uncommon occurrence. In some provinces such vigorous measures have been taken that apparently the period of ten years will not be required to suppress the traffic. In the Province of Shansi, for example, the raising of the poppy is absolutely prohibited. Travelers in the Province of Szechwan have recently reported that they saw no signs of the poppy there and that the opium dens were closed. Lord William Cecil testifies that, whereas when he was in China in 1907, he found the country between Hankow and Harbin "beautiful with white and pink crops of poppy," in 1909 he did not see a single poppy flower while traversing the same country. Few in the West realize what a vast and revolutionary change this abolition of the opium traffic is. It involves the reorganization of the entire fiscal system, but the Government has gone forward regardless of financial considerations. The Chinese themselves have been, and are, the leaders in this movement, and it is significant that one of the most effective advocates of the suppression of opium, at the meetings of the International Opium Commission recently held in Shanghai, was Tong Kaison, a Chinese Christian. When one considers the number of people involved, the strength of the habit combated, and the results already attained, this anti-opium crusade is one of the greatest moral movements of modern times. It is being conducted with an aggressiveness and with a degree of success which puts to shame the progress of temperance and certain other moral movements in Western lands. Changes like these seem almost incredible when one reflects on the constitution of the Chinese mind and its unchanging attitude throughout the centuries.

China's awakening is not only in industrial enterprise, political reform, and social progress; unquestionably the greatest changes in China are those pertaining to education, and out of this a new spirit in the Chinese people is resulting. Literally thousands of Chinese students have been sent abroad to study. In 1900 there were less than a score of Chinese students studying in Tokyo. At present there are not less than four thousand there, and at one time, in 1907, the number was as high as fifteen thousand. While the number studying in Japan has declined, the number going to America and Europe is steadily increasing. There are now in the different universities and schools of the United States not less than six hundred Chinese students, and plans have been perfected for sending thither in the near future a much larger number. There are also about five hundred studying in Great Britain and on the Continent. In the history of education there has been no such extensive migration of students from one country to other lands. At the time when Japan had the largest number of her youth studying abroad there were only about 1700 in America and a much smaller number in Europe. Another striking fact in connection with the Chinese student migration is that the largest number who have gone abroad to study have come from the most reactionary province—the Province of Hunan, the one which longest resisted the introduction of the telegraph.

Even more remarkable than the sending abroad for study of her own young men and young women, has been the rapid transformation of the system of education in China. In 1905, by one stroke of the vermilion pencil, the Empress Dowager abolished completely and forever the competitive examination system which had been in operation for two thousand years. The old examination halls are already falling into ruins or have been torn down to make way for modern schools. The Imperial Government has issued in five volumes a complete set of regulations which include a curriculum of studies based largely upon that of Japan, which is in turn based on American and European models. Within the last five years the Imperial Government has not only sent educational commissions to Europe and America to make a careful study of the educational systems of the West, but has also taken to heart the results of their investigations. An increasing number of American and European educators have been invited by provincial and municipal governments, as well as by Chinese gentry, to help to establish modern institutions of learning in different parts of the country. A far larger number of Japanese teachers have been secured for the same purpose. It is estimated that at one time there were as many as one thousand Japanese co-operating in the educational reforms throughout China. Modern schools and colleges are springing up like mushrooms all over China. In the Province of Chihli there are already scores of thousands of students and scholars in these modern institutions. In Peking alone there are 200 i.-

stitutions with 17,000 students. In each of four other
cities in China there are already over 10,000 students
of modern learning. Scores of girls' schools have
sprung up in the different parts of China, and nothing
in the general awakening of the country is more mo-
mentous than this change in the status and education
of women.

Many schools, both for men and for women, have
insufficient staffs of teachers and therefore are doing
superficial work. It is a case of the blind leading the
blind. Many mistakes are being made and much
money is being wasted, but the significant fact is that
China has determined to give Western education to
her millions of youth. To realize the meaning of the
educational revolution, one need only recall that Japan
now has nearly six millions of youth in her schools
and colleges, and that the same proportion will some
day give China over fifty millions. The day is coming,
and that very soon, when China will have more students than any other nation of the world.

China, then, is in the midst of an intellectual revolution, but at present her education has a pronouncedly
utilitarian end. Her one motive and desire is that she
may acquire the secret of the industrial, commercial,
financial, military, and naval power of the West. This
is her deliberate purpose and she is succeeding in a
marked degree. Is there not something ominous in a
nation of 400,000,000 people moving forward into
modern civilization with no higher motive than this?

Siam is in a condition of metamorphosis. Under the
enlightened rule of King Chulalongkorn I, she has

been open to Western culture in a remarkable manner. Wonderful progress has been made in all branches of administration; even compulsory education has been introduced, the government system of schools being in the most promising condition. Recent economic, social, and educational changes throughout the Philippine Islands as well as in British Malaya and the Dutch East Indies are striking examples of modern progress in the midst of exceedingly difficult conditions.

Persia also is sharing in the general awakening of the East and is undergoing a transformation. The movement there seeks primarily to establish civil freedom and ensure social progress, and the immediate aim is to set up a constitutional and popular form of government. The fact that it has that particular aim makes its leaders regard such nations as the United States and England as specially worthy of imitation, and the example of these nations and of Japan has impressed them with the conviction that national progress and effectiveness are impossible without education, science, and civilization. Consequently, there is a new and growing demand for education in sciences and in Western languages. Schools for giving this education are springing up all over the country, and there is a great anxiety to learn. Over and over again, men come to the missionary with the appeal, " We are ignorant and know nothing, and you must be our teacher." In Persia, the old régime is passing away and the new is being formed. Nothing is fixed as yet, but in the Near East as well as in the Far East, events are moving with a rapidity that is nothing short of marvelous, and we cannot tell what a few years may bring forth.

Even in Turkestan and Afghanistan the modern spirit of transformation and change is felt. It is inevitable that amid all the restless movements in the neighboring countries — Persia, India, and Turkey — Central Asia and Afghanistan will not remain dormant. There are many indications of the influence of the modern currents of the more distant parts of the East also being felt in these regions. Nothing can hold back the advance of Western civilization into the very heart of Asia. The railway and caravan are forcing upon the people through every pass and along every channel of communication some of the latest inventions of our time. At Kabul, one may see sewing-machines, rifles with smokeless powder, gramophones, and automobiles. One of the results of the visit of the Amir of Afghanistan to India was the arrangement by him for the erection of looms in his capital, and now we hear of the transportation by camel train of pianos and motor cars, and apparatus for wireless telegraphy through the Khaiber Pass. For the management of all these modern industries, a staff of European engineers and mechanics has been admitted into the country.

India, in common with all other lands in the East, is in a state of change and unrest. Great and surprising transformations have taken place in the past few years, changes which many did not expect to see occur until another quarter of a century had elapsed. Among these one notes the growing sense of concern on the part of many outside the missionary and Christian community over the ills which afflict the great masses of the people of this land—ills intellectual, social, and religious. Quite apart from the political movement and agitation throughout India the multitudes are in the midst of marked social and industrial developments and transformations. It is true that there are large areas of country inhabitated by scores of millions of agricultural people, who are as yet largely untouched by the new spirit of change and progress, but the significant fact is, that the higher and more influential classes have been profoundly affected by it. These classes and castes, which for ages have had undisputed authority in India, are now seeking with eagerness to increase their efficiency and to broaden their power. The educated Hindus, and increasingly the educated Mohammedans, have naturally been most profoundly influenced by the modern civilization as a result of their knowledge of the English language and their contact with the outside world. It is remarkable also that individuals from the lowest castes and from the outcastes are, under the influence of Christianity and education, emerging from their inferior position in Indian society, and are aspiring to places of prominence and influence. Morever, there are unmistakable signs in different parts of India of the break-up of the system of caste, which has done more to hold back the progress of Indian society and to hinder the advance of Christianity than any other cause.

Even more remarkable and encouraging is the thirst

for learning on the part of the women of India. The last Government Quinquennial Report on the Progress of Education in India, for 1902–1907, in giving the percentage of girls in school to the population of school-going age, places Burma at the top of the list with 8.14 per cent. Bombay comes next with 5.9. The Punjab has 2.6, and the United Provinces only 1.2. It would appear that for the whole country not one girl in twenty-five of school-going age is in school, and that the overwhelming proportion of those who are do not advance beyond the lower primary grade. There is, however, a growing desire among the men for the education of their daughters, wives, and sisters. Without doubt India is undergoing great social, political, industrial, and religious changes. A new nation is coming to birth.

Of no other country in the recent or remote past could it be said so truly as it can be said of Turkey, that it is a nation born in a day. On July 24, 1908, the reactionary Sultan Abdul Hamid, who had reigned since 1876, was forced by the progressive party of young Turks to grant a constitution and call a parliament. The marvelous change came unexpectedly and with lightning-like rapidity. No correspondent, missionary, consul, or ambassador had predicted it. In some respects it was the most extraordinary revolution which has ever taken place among either an Asiatic or a European people. Within the course of a few weeks Turkey passed from the most absolute despotism to one of the progressive countries of the world. The Young Turks carried all with them, from the Christian races, the Jews, and even uncivilized tribes, to many of the Mohammedan leaders and parts of the army, and won the sympathetic and enthusiastic approval of every foreign nation. Abdul Hamid has finally been deposed and succeeded by Mehmed V, a man of liberal views.

The peacefulness and moderation characterizing the first stage of this revolution, that of the summer of 1908, were as notable as its suddenness and completeness. All admit that the Young Turks at that time showed great restraint, poise, and ability. Many predicted a day of terrible retribution, should those who had suffered under the old government ever get the reins of power into their own hands. Moreover, the reactionary movement of the spring of 1909 seemed to afford additional justification for such forebodings, but although terrible bloodshed and cruelty characterized that awful ebullition of religious fanaticism and reactionary jealousy in Cilicia, subsequent events have clearly shown that the progressive forces which, under the leadership of the Young Turk party accomplished the early revolution and are still in the ascendant, are of such strength and influence as to give promise of leading the movement of progress from strength to strength.

Although the Turkish revolution took place so recently, the changes which it has accomplished seem almost incredible. The autocracy has been done away with, a constitutional government has been established, the once forbidden words, " Liberty, equality, fraternity, justice," the proclaiming of which a few years

THE FIRST TURKISH PARLIAMENT

ago would have sent a man into banishment or to death, are now freely spoken. The system of spies, in connection with which there were said to have been over 40,000 in Constantinople alone, has been abolished. The galling restrictions of the censorship have been removed. The freest agitation of political questions is permitted in the press and in public meetings.

Interesting educational changes are taking place. Under the old régime, knowledge was dangerous and men hid it. Now, it is coming to light. Meetings for the discussion of all sorts of questions, political and otherwise, are held in mosques and churches, in halls and public squares. The number of periodicals has already been greatly multiplied. It is said that over two hundred new papers have been started in Constantinople alone. The changes are affecting powerfully the social life. There could be no better indication of this than the changing position of women. The general ignorance and social degradation of Mohammedan women had been one of the greatest barriers to the advance of Turkey. The new movement carries with it the education and emancipation of women. No one three years ago would have dreamed of Turkish women attending public meetings, but that is a common practice now.

In the case of Turkey—as of every nation which has traveled along the road of progress—there will come times of reaction. The problem of popular government in Turkey is by no means solved. Old jealousies and rivalries will continue to assert themselves; but whatever reaction there may be, Turkey will never go

back where she was before July 24, 1908. And say
what we may about the future, the present, at least,
is a time of liberty. There has come at last throughout
the Turkish Empire freedom to travel, to assemble, to
speak, to print, to educate. Only some great loosening
of the principles and prejudices of the Mohammedan
past could have permitted such a transformation, even
though it were to prove but a temporary change. It
is more than doubtful whether Islam ever can supply
a moral sense of sufficient power to sustain these new
principles of liberty. The Turkish people, too, have
moved in response to the flowing tide and have shown
that they, like the other nations, are ready now to
learn from the Christian civilizations of the West.
What the future of the New Turkey will be depends
entirely upon what she is taught during this time of
open-mindedness and change.

It is not necessary to call attention to the economic,
social, and educational development of the native races
of South Africa, which development, along with the
political evolution, has advanced steadily through the
past two or three generations. Suffice it to state that
in no period has the progress been more marked,
judged by every test, than during the last two decades.
This progress is observable in almost every part of
what is known as the Sub-Continent, the part of Africa
lying south of the Zambesi.

The facts regarding the transformation of Egypt
during the last two or three decades are also well
known. The industrial and educational advances
which have been made within this period have been

indeed marked. Egypt, formerly one of the worst
governed countries of modern times, has now a government which may be characterized as stable, enlightened, and efficient. The transformations which have
taken place in the Upper Nile portion of the Sudan
within the last five years constitute one of the most
encouraging examples of progress to be found in any
part of the non-Christian world. Good railways and
roads have been made; modern methods of agriculture
and forestry have been introduced; industries have
been established; a sound financial system has been
put into operation; the country is administered with
justice; a good school system, leading up to the
efficient Gordon College, has been created; social evils
have been abolished, including slavery and polygamy.
No region had sunk to a lower depth, socially and
economically, yet few sections of the non-Christian
world give brighter signs of promise.

Even in the great heart of Africa the streams of
modern progress are moving with increasing momentum. Only a generation ago, at the time when Stanley
met Livingstone, the vast region of Central Africa,
covering a territory of over two million square miles,
was practically unknown. An examination of the map
of Africa of that time indicates there a blank with the
exception of the coast lines. In the intervening years
that whole region has been explored and is now well
known, and the new maps show the river systems,
mountains, lakes, cities, and towns. This whole region
is now divided among European powers, and is coming
into the light of civilization. Thirty years ago there

were no railways in this great territory. Now 1200 miles of railway are in operation, and 1000 miles more are under construction. It took Stanley 104 days to make the journey from the East Coast to Victoria Nyanza, whereas it can now be made by rail in comfort within three days. Railways lead toward the heart of Africa, not only from the East Coast, but also from the west, the north, and the south. About twenty years ago, in Uganda, the only avenues of communication were footpaths. Now broad roads, on which the Governor is able to use his motor car, intersect the country in every direction. On the inland rivers and lakes, the steamer lines cover a distance of nearly 7000 miles. In this territory also over 5000 miles of telegraph are in operation. A modern postal service is extending in every principal division of interior Africa. Bishop Tucker has pointed out that when he first reached Uganda they were obliged to wait eight or nine months for a home mail, but now there is a weekly service. In the year 1907, the mails of British East Africa and of the Congo carried three million letters and parcels.

Educational progress is also evident. Not a few tribes and peoples have within a generation acquired a written language and the beginning of a literature. Many hundreds, if not thousands, of schools under government and missionary auspices, may now be found throughout this expanse, where at the time of Livingstone's journeys there were none. In Uganda alone there are in these schools over 30,000 boys and girls. There are also large sales of school-books and

Christian literature in the vernaculars. With the exception of the Belgian Congo with its terrible abuses and parts of French Africa in which an unprogressive policy is maintained, the advancement of interior Africa has been of such extent and character as to constitute a ground for great hopefulness for the future. It reveals the larger part of a vast continent in the beginnings of transformation from ignorance, barbarism, and superstition, into the light of modern civilization, and as time advances the transformation will become more and more complete. Owing to the simpler character of the primitive African peoples, this continent is in many respects the most plastic part of the world, and will be during this generation the most readily susceptible to whatever influences are brought to bear upon it.

Out of these remarkable movements among the nations one feature emerges, so noticeable and important as to merit special consideration. At first, these changes which are taking place were largely involuntary, and, in many cases, were forced upon unwilling peoples, but now they are becoming part of a definite policy of national aggrandizement. Since the war between Japan and Russia, in all parts of the non-Christian world, but especially in Asia, this national spirit has been growing, and, associated with it, a spirit of racial pride and antagonism. In almost every country it is the expression of the growing self-consciousness of the people. They are learning to be proud of their past. They believe that they have resources and ability to make their own contribution to the life of

the world. They wish to preserve their individuality
and independence and to be true to their own national
and racial characteristics. They are beginning to
feel that they have a right to stand alongside of the
great nations of the West, not as inferiors but as
equals. Accordingly they resent all foreign domina-
tion and are sensitive as to the influence of all things
foreign. They wish to be allowed to work out their
own destiny, and are forming high conceptions of
what that destiny is. They are becoming more and
more ambitious and confident in their own powers
and ability, and are no longer willing to move quietly
on, but are determined to succeed and become great
and independent.

There are many illustrations of the growth of this
spirit of nationalism in the non-Christian world. We
have seen how it has manifested itself in emancipating
Japan by sheer force of merit from an extra-territorial
position among nations and finally in making her the
dominant power in the East. In China there is now
another marked example of growing consciousness of
nationality and of a desire to acquire national independence and power. We find this spirit exhibiting
itself in various ways. One of the viceroys has prepared a book on patriotism which has been circulated
by the hundreds of thousands of copies—more than
any other book save the Scriptures. Many articles
bearing on the subject of nationalism are appearing in
Chinese periodicals. There are frequent references to
" our country " in the newspapers and in speeches.
The use of the Chinese flag on modern school build-

A CHINESE COLLIERY CENTER—1000 MILES FROM THE SEA

ings and the singing of patriotic songs in the schools are other illustrations. Societies have been formed to debate political questions, especially the relation of China to other nations. The boycott against American and other foreign goods, the creation of a modern army, now numbering over 200,000 men, and the riots occurring from time to time, are also facts pointing eloquently and unmistakably to the expansion of the national spirit.

Not less significant is the attitude to Christianity adopted by some of the leading Chinese reformers, who have been imperfectly instructed. The awakening of a national spirit in China tends to close minds and hearts to everything connected with the foreign teacher. Without doubt the officials are indirectly doing much to prevent the people from accepting Christianity. Apparently they cannot free their minds from the conviction that the missionary movement is after all only another form of political activity. They have had experience in the past with certain forms of Christianity, particularly the Roman Catholic, which abundantly explains the strength of their conviction. It is not strange, therefore, that it is openly announced in Chinese newspapers that the programme of the New China must be to recover China's sovereign rights and to extinguish the Church. China fears any teaching or movement which centers abroad. Her sentiment is no more against Christianity than against railways and mines worked or superintended by foreigners. In fact, she is more eager to redeem her railways and mines than to expel Christians. The spirit of restiveness under dominant foreign influence manifests itself, further, not only in the political and commercial relations of China, but also inside the Chinese Christian Church itself. At conferences in three of the principal cities, attended by the leading Chinese pastors and Christian teachers, one of the chief reasons given by them to explain why more of the ablest Christian students do not enter the ministry, was the strong feeling of dissatisfaction with the subordinate position held by native pastors.

In India also there is an equally evident example of growing national spirit. The Swadeshi (*i.e.* our own country) Movement which has developed to such an extent in recent years is a direct outcome or exhibition of nationalism. On the industrial side, it has led to the formation of Swadeshi commercial companies, Swadeshi factories and mills, Swadeshi steamship lines, and Swadeshi banks. All of these are organized, financed, and directed by Indians and have been managed with commendable efficiency. They are usually conducted along modern lines, and represent a serious effort on the part of the Indian people to improve their industrial position, to increase their industrial efficiency, and to make their country industrially and commercially independent. An illustration of the progressive character of this development is the fact that an Indian society has been formed in connection with which scores of promising Indian young men have been sent to various European countries as well as to America and Japan to master certain trades and industrial processes, in order that they may on their return lead their countrymen out into a more effective and productive economic life.

Many Indian reviews and other periodicals have been started within recent years to promote the development of the Indian national or patriotic spirit, some of which are edited with ability and exert a wide influence. Even the Indian papers which are most loyal to the Government are devoted more than ever to the discussion of such questions. An immense amount of literature is being published in a very cheap form, both in the vernaculars and in English, treating the social, industrial, and political aspects of nationalism, and this literature is being circulated broadcast in all parts of India. The Indian National Congress, as heretofore, devotes itself largely to the discussion of the political phases of the national movement, and within the past few years, an increasing number of provincial and district conferences have been held for the purpose of discussing and agitating similar questions. The recent acts of violence, although limited to a very small section of Indian society, may be regarded as unfortunate exhibitions of the same national spirit. Among the masses there is a growing feeling that they should be treated with more consideration and justice by Europeans. This feeling has shown itself, as it did not even ten years ago, in bitter complaints concerning any unjust treatment in railway trains, on steamships, and also on plantations and in offices. Even in the Christian Church this independence and rebellion against unequal treatment is manifested. There is a keen feeling of dissatisfaction with reference to the government of the Churches, and the Indians are strongly demanding that they have a more responsible part. So much do they resent their present subordination, that the feeling has often become anti-missionary. Rather than be subject to a foreigner, they are sometimes content to be without his help.

Africa as well as Asia affords illustrations of a growing national and racial patriotism. Nationalism in Egypt is in most respects a pro-Moslem movement and therefore intensifies the dislike of the Egyptian towards the foreigner and the Christian. It tends to fan the flames of fanaticism, both in the cities and in the provinces, and this makes it much more dangerous than it is in other parts of the world. In South Africa the movement may be characterized as racial rather than national. Among the native Christians it manifested itself in a special way, known as the Ethiopian Movement. This was an effort to establish an African Church independent of the control or supervision of foreign missionaries, and it attracted to itself some of the loyal and genuine Christians as well as those who were disaffected and unworthy. It served to undermine the former trust of the colored people in white missionaries and eventually, through becoming entangled in politics, resulted in such dangerous tendencies as to call forth repressive governmental measures. As a result of lax practice with regard to baptism and the want of searching church discipline, the movement has declined in spiritual power and no longer wields its former influence. Owing to various causes there has been a growing antagonism between the white and the black races in South Africa, outside as well as within the Church. New racial hopes have been stimulated in the hearts of the people of South Africa even by so remote a cause as the victories of the Japanese, and besides this, some of the regulations and disciplinary measures employed by different colonial governments have served to drive the colored people definitely into the arms of the Mohammedans and have brought about a fraternization involving political as well as religious danger. The war in German Southwest Africa has also embittered the feelings of the Cape colored people against everything European, while the antagonism of race and color has recently been rendered more serious, inasmuch as the new Constitution of the Union of South Africa withdraws from the colored people certain rights hitherto tacitly conceded to them, and because the Parliament of the Union has the power to deprive the colored people of further privileges. This retrogressive action has stirred the feelings of the half-castes to the depths, and has kindled a fire which cannot easily be extinguished.

It is difficult to specify the causes of these great upheavals in all these countries. The leaven of Western civilization has for many years been slowly penetrating the Asiatic consciousness and what is now coming to light is largely the result of this process. It has been greatly accelerated, however, by the growing commercial intercourse of to-day, the streams of travel between East and West, and the migrations of students. We cannot exaggerate, for example, the influence upon

China of the return of Chinese students from Tokyo
and the West, with their minds full of science and
Western methods, but their hearts burning because of
what they have learned of the Opium War with England, and of what they regard as the unjust exclusion
acts of America, Canada, and Australia, of the seizing
of their territory by Russia, Germany, France, and
Japan, and of the building in their own capital city of
legations, which are like fortresses, stocked with
munitions of war and manned with foreign troops.
The ascendancy of the West, so bitter to the Asiatic,
has emphasized the value of a new and better conception of nationality.   The progress, victory, and power
of the Empire of the Rising Sun have become known
and have been discussed in the marts of China, the
bazaars of India, the khans of Persia and Turkey,
and even in the caravansaries of Arabia and Africa,
and have powerfully stimulated national hopes and
ambitions and led to great changes in national outlook
and practice.   As a writer in *The Spectator* has pointed out, " By some inscrutable means of temperamental
communication, the aspirations of one country are
quickly adopted by another, however different in intellectual and political equipment they may be."   Even
so Japan's ambitions and successes have kindled like
aspirations in other lands and have led to this restless movement and this conscious copying of the West.

But a far more potent cause has been the sense of
the value of the individual and the desire for genuine
liberty and progress which have been awakened and
developed in men through the knowledge of the

Christian Scriptures, through the proclamation of the mission of Christ to man, and through the Christ-leavened institutions, ideals, and practices of the West. It is this discovery of the worth and rights of the individual man that has made possible, for example, the ignoring of caste by such numbers of the educated classes in India, and it is this which alone has caused the movement among the native races in Africa. In many lands the Christian missionary has been the pioneer of all the subsequent development, and wherever Christ has come, He has led men to look up to new ideals and to set new values on things. This goes far towards explaining the origin of the whole movement. The Chinese, the Indian, and the African are seeking to shape their nations to achieve great destinies, because they are learning from the West the lesson which Christ taught it, the dignity and inherent greatness of every human life, and are realizing thereby what they can become. Without doubt, as in Korea, so in many another land, Christianity has furnished the principal transforming influence and power.

What is to be the future of these nations? This question forces itself upon us as we survey the facts. In every part of the non-Christian world this is a time of transition. The nations are passing from the old to the new, and everywhere they are looking to the West for guidance. What guidance are they to receive? The Chinese are anxious to secure all the material advantages of Western civilization, while ignoring its underlying principles and inspiration. Japan has adopted Western methods in everything that will in-

crease her material power. Is this all that India and
Turkey and all these other lands are to find when they
look towards the West? They are examining us to
see what has made us rich and powerful, and there is
a grave danger that they may form wrong judgments.
Religion is the most fundamental thing in our civilization, but there is an undoubted danger that these
peoples may not recognize this truth to-day. They
have been taking much from us. If we do not give
them our religion, have we given them of our best?
If they adopt our civilization without our religion,
what moral disasters may not result? Have not,
therefore, Christian people a special responsibility at
such time as this?

The responsibility is increased by the fact that these
peoples will not always remain open to new influences.
The words of Bishop Lefroy, of Lahore, are doubtless
applicable not only to India, but also to practically all
of the other non-Christian lands which have been considered. "Of this we may be certain, that unless at
the present time, while almost everything is in solution, and the direction largely undetermined, Christianity really enters in as a potent factor, able in greater or
less degree to exercise that commanding influence
which is hers by right, if only she is given a chance;
and if the new life of India is allowed to set and take
shape and form, independently of her influence, then
for generations to come the door to advance will be
fast-barred to a degree of which we have hitherto had
no experience whatever." The need of a strong religious basis for public and individual life is so urgent

that unless met in a satisfactory way by the Christian Church the great majority of the one million or more educated Indians will inevitably drift into some form or other of Hindu pantheism or rationalistic theism, which will then constitute the most serious obstacle in the way of the spread of Christianity. Moreover, now is the opportunity in China to impress upon the officials and the people of that land, that only righteousness and integrity of character can make a nation permanently great, and that these are the direct products of the Christian Gospel. It cannot be said that vacillation is a characteristic of the Chinese. If a race with their traits determine on a certain attitude toward religion, the danger is that they may not change again for generations. We have to face the certainty that, in a comparatively short space of time, this stage of transition will have passed. The present plastic condition of the nations will have given place to a condition of rigidity, and the influences which might be so effective if brought to bear now, will then be exerted in vain.

The development and spread of the spirit of national and racial patriotism is, however, the most significant fact of all. It is not an evil thing. It cannot and should not be checked. Christ never by teaching or example resisted or withstood the spirit of true nationalism. Wherever His principles, including those pertaining to the supreme claims of His Kingdom on earth, have had the right of way, they have served to strengthen national spirit and not to weaken it. But it is a matter of profound concern to the Western world. Who can measure what it will mean for man-

kind when not only Japan but also China with her un-
limited resources, and India with her 300,000,000
people take their place among the great civilized
powers? The influence which they will exert upon
the life and thought of the world must be enormous,
whatever its nature; whether it will be Christian or
not depends largely on the direction given to it to-day.
It is the duty of the Church to bring pure Christianity
to bear at once in order to help to educate, purify,
unify, guide, and strengthen the national spirit. The
possibilities are great if the Christian Church will
identify itself freely and largely with all these noble
national aspirations. If Christianity will show that it
has a message not merely for individuals but for
society and for the nation as a whole, that it can
adapt itself to the people whom it seeks to save, and
that it does not deem it essential, even desirable,
that the ordered life of the Christian community in
Asia and Africa should follow in every respect the
lines of European and American Christianity, it may
attract instead of repel these rising nations. Their
newly found life when ruled by Christ will be a source
of strength to their own nations and to the Christian
faith.

CRITICAL TENDENCIES AND
INFLUENCES IN THE
NON-CHRISTIAN WORLD

CHAPTER II

CRITICAL TENDENCIES AND INFLUENCES IN THE
NON-CHRISTIAN WORLD

THE changes and transformations that are in progress
in these non-Christian nations are not confined to the
political, social, and commercial spheres, but are affecting the religious also, and that in two quite opposite
directions. On the one hand, by the removing of old
prejudices, the way is unmistakably being prepared for
the acceptance of Christianity by large masses of the
people in many lands, and in this aspect all that is happening is full of hope. These movements towards
Christianity and the opportunity presented by them
will be considered in the next chapter, but here it may
be well to make a survey of the special difficulties which
Christianity has to meet in the present situation.
We turn, therefore, in this chapter to observe that,
there are certain tendencies, movements, and influences
manifesting themselves in various countries, which are
not only tending to close these nations against Christianity, but are placing in danger their moral and religious future. Prominent among these are the cor-
rupting influences associated with Western civilization
which are permeating many parts of the non-Christian
world. Just as the development of improved means

of communication has greatly facilitated the propagation of the Gospel and the sending forth of the pure and hopeful influences of Western civilization, so the drawing together of the nations and races as a result of these improvements has made possible the more rapid spread of influences antagonistic to the extension of Christ's Kingdom. They have familiarized a vast and increasing number of non-Christian peoples with the worst practices of Western life. In every port, as well as in many interior cities of non-Christian nations, one finds concentrated the evil influences of the West. Scattered throughout Africa and the Pacific Islands, not to mention other sections of the world, are thousands of Western traders, large numbers of whom are exerting a demoralizing influence. It is most unfortunate that the European settlers who are traveling inland in the various colonies and protectorates, as well as the agents of trading companies, though belonging to nominally Christian nations, are far too often men who, in their characters and lives, misrepresent Christianity. Testimony is borne also by many to the corrupt influence of Japanese merchants and immigrants in Korea, Manchuria, and China, who are also regarded as representing in a measure the civilization of the West.

The multiplying of points of contact with the West, through the expansion of its commercial and industrial system, has introduced among non-Christian peoples new temptations. It is a great misfortune that commercial enterprise, without pure Christianity, communicates to the people an added hardening of heart, a materializing of life, and a new immorality. With the influx of European civilization into Africa, for example, there seems to have come a flood of pernicious influences, of vice, and of disease. It is commented upon by many observers, that whenever an Eastern and a Western nation impinge upon each other, the contact in some mysterious way tends to bring out the worst there is in each. The vices of Western life seem to work with added deadliness among men of the more simple civilizations, such as those found in Africa, in Oceania, and in parts of Asia. This can be observed in the debasing influence on native character and life of the mining centers, to which many thousands of African, Chinese, and Indian laborers have been taken; but the great instance is the increase in the liquor traffic, which is traceable directly to the West.

It would be difficult to mention a part of the non-Christian world where the liquor traffic is not increasing, but its most fearful ravages are to be found in the ports and hinterland of Africa. The Anglican and Roman Catholic bishops in different parts of Africa bear testimony both to the spread of this traffic and also to its demoralizing influence. Special public attention has recently been called to this subject as a result of the discussion evoked by the Report of the Government Committee regarding the Liquor Traffic in Southern Nigeria. In the year 1908, over three million gallons of spirits were imported into Southern Nigeria, valued at about one-fourth of the value of the total imports of that colony. It is significant that

liquor is often used for currency. Drunkenness is
very prevalent in different parts of the colony, especially in those most exposed to European influence,
Not only the men, but also the women and the children
are addicted to it, and it is said that in many places
possibly the women drink more than the men. Bishop
Johnson recently told of visiting a school of seventy-
five children between the ages of eight and sixteen,
where on inquiry he found that only fifteen of them
had not been drinking gin. The desire for drink has
become so dominating that cases are not infrequent of
parents pawning their children to get money to spend
for liquor. Bishop Oluwole gave testimony before the
Government Committee of Inquiry, in 1909, to having
seen a girl pawned for $37. One of the most striking
indications of the spread of the liquor traffic is the fact
that even Mohammedans have become addicted to in-
temperance. Facts similar to these about Nigeria
could be given with reference to many of the other
colonies and protectorates of Africa. Among the
Pacific Islands too, while the situation has improved
in some of them, there are other groups where the
liquor traffic is exerting as deadly an influence as in
any part of Africa. One of the most damaging and
serious facts of all, is that, for purposes of revenue,
this traffic is often directly promoted by colonial governments, and in other cases is conducted with their
connivance or tacit approval.

The most flagrant example of a so-called Christian
government using its power and machinery directly to
defraud, to oppress, and to degrade native races be-

cause of greed, is that of Belgium in its relation to the Congo. On the unimpeachable testimony of foreign missionaries and travelers, and even of members of the Commission appointed by the Belgian Government to investigate conditions, there is still in operation in the Belgian Congo a system of organized oppression and plunder, in order to increase the output of rubber and other products for the benefit of a commercial company, which is only a covering name for the Belgian State. The land of the people has been largely taken in violation of communal and tribal rights. The people have been reduced to misery. For the profit of the State they have been and still are forced to gather the products of the land thus taken from them, and the pay granted is miserably poor. No refusal is allowed, and the most diabolical methods have been employed by the subordinate agents of the State to enforce obedience. Homes are broken up as a result of members being forcibly taken away and compelled to go into the forests to gather rubber. Father Yer-meerseh sums up the condition of great numbers of the inhabitants in the words, " immeasurable misery." Without doubt, under the old régime which obtained at the time of Stanley's last visit, before the European influence became dominant, the tribes were infinitely happier and more prosperous than at the present time. It is hoped that under the new king of Belgium necessary reforms may be effected.

It is a sad, but inevitable fact, that as a rule the masses of non-Christian people, and even many of their leaders, do not discriminate between the genuine

Christians who come from Western countries, such as missionaries and sincere and worthy Christian laymen in commercial and government pursuits, and the vicious representatives of the West who go among them. It is not strange, therefore, that the following challenge is a typical expression of the opinion of a great multitude of Asiatics and Africans: " You come to us with your religion. You degrade our people with drink. You scorn our religion, in many points like your own, and then you wonder why Christianity makes such slow progress among us. I will tell you. It is because you are not like your Christ."

These degrading influences constitute a deadly gift from the modern civilization of the West, but it is still worse to have to recognize that some of them are carried to the East also by numbers of its own sons. The increasing number of travelers from non-Christian nations, especially the wonderful migration of Oriental students to America and Europe, has, in many cases, resulted in exposing these more enterprising representatives of the non-Christian world to the materialistic, antichristian, and demoralizing sides of the life of Western nations. On their return, some of them, as teachers, editors, and government officials, constitute a great barrier to the spread of the Gospel. This has been notably true of many Chinese and Korean students on their return from Japan. In Japan old ideals have been completely destroyed under the influence of the West, and no adequate new ideal has been generally adopted. As a consequence the moral tone is low, and many of those who go to Japan to study fall victims to the prevailing looseness and carry back this attitude to their native land. Moreover, there is a danger that the thousands of Japanese teachers who are going into Korea, Manchuria, and China will be apostles of materialism instead of being helpful in influencing the people in favor of higher things. In addition to what is being forced upon China by the West, there is at her very doors this menace to her highest welfare.

Attention should also be called to the effects resulting from the spread of infidel and rationalistic ideas and materialistic views. From many parts of the non-Christian world have come reports telling of the wide dissemination of agnostic, atheistic, materialistic, and destructive socialistic literature, traceable to Western sources. The stream of this influence is flowing over China to-day, both directly from the West and also by way of Japan. The writings of Haeckel, Huxley, and Spencer, and anti-theistic and antichristian articles, both original and translated from European magazines, are widely circulated not only in India and Japan, but also in such newly awakened countries as Turkey and China. The periodicals of the non-Christian religions are active and aggressive in publishing articles showing supposed mistakes in the Bible and the conclusions of destructive criticism. Ingersoll and Bradlaugh are extensively quoted in pamphlets against the Christian faith, and the most bitter and absurd arguments against Christianity in which these men ever indulged have been translated into the vernaculars of India, and have been disseminated even among the villages. Agnostic literature has been systematically introduced among students and in the public libraries. Indecent French literature has been widely circulated, especially in the Far East and Near East. All this is having its effect in unsettling men's minds and in making them hostile to the reception of Christianity.

The unsettling process has been greatly quickened and emphasized by the spread of modern secular education. In the two most advanced non-Christian nations, Japan and India, there are to-day great government systems of education, including hundreds of thousands of pupils and students. China and Korea are rapidly establishing similar systems, and that of China alone will soon number its pupils and students by the million. With the exception of those of the mission schools and colleges of India which are aided by Government, these systems are throughout pronouncedly secular. The governments of Turkey, Persia, Egypt, and other non-Christian countries are also rapidly developing secular educational institutions, and from these Christian teaching is excluded as a matter of course.

In Japan the government system of education, which embraces nearly all of the educational work of the country, has undermined belief in the old faiths, and, as a result, the rising generation is almost without religion. The educated portion of the population is thus largely materialistic and agnostic. The system of moral instruction in the government schools tends, on the one hand, to ignore or even to create contempt

BUILDINGS OF THE UNIVERSITY OF CALCUTTA

for religion, or, on the other hand, to regard nationalism as a substitute for religion. Few of the government school educators have any use for religion.
Hence a process is going on which will make it increasingly difficult for the Gospel to find entrance to the
minds of the educated Japanese. The text-books in
these modern institutions are indifferent, if not actually hostile, to religion. The men educated in the government schools under non-Christian or hostile influence thus drift into agnosticism and materialism and
become a great menace to the Church.

In Korea, the activity of the Japanese Government
in establishing schools all through the land, and the
hunger of the Korean people after any kind of knowledge will result soon in the education, to an extent
hitherto unknown, of large numbers of young men.
It is feared that they will become a menace rather than
a blessing to the nation, because the education which
they are receiving through the government institutions
is planting rationalistic ideas in the minds of the hitherto simple-minded people. This may make it more difficult for them to adopt a new religion.

In China the enormous spread of government education, usually antichristian, is rapidly producing a class
of intelligent objectors to the Gospel. Until recently
most of those opposed to religion were ignorant, and
it was comparatively easy to meet their difficulties.
But now " Science without Christianity " is the watch-
word of many students. The aspiration for new
learning seems to be fixing the minds of the Chinese
upon the materialistic aspects of our modern civiliza-

tion. They accept quickly the agnostic explanations of the universe, and are apt to receive the impression that religion is not necessary to the life of a nation. When through the study of science they see the folly of their old superstitions they will give them up, as they are by nature an eminently practical people, and, unless influenced by Christianity, will be apt to put nothing in their place.

The Anglo-Indian system of education in India has afforded a degree of Western culture to several hundreds of thousands of Indian students. In its higher grades each year its influence is being brought to bear upon scores of thousands. The members of this educated class will affect profoundly the future of India, forming as they do the connecting link between the British rulers and the mass of the Indian population, while from their ranks come a disproportionate number of the great army of officials and leaders of popular modern thought. They are exposed, and in most cases fall victims to those agnostic, materialistic, and antichristian influences which come from the West.

A recent writer in the *Church Missionary Review* thus emphasizes the peril associated with the modern education now being afforded Indian youth. "We look abroad and see what is the condition of those nations where religion and education are wholly dissociated, and mark the results. As Herbert Spencer has said, ' The growth of intellectualization in advance of moralization has done enormous mischief.' I am one of those who believe that most of the unrest and discontent in India arises from the faults of our purely secular educational system. For, be it remembered, while there is no religious or moral teaching at the government school, there is none in the home either." Pandita Ramabai lays equal emphasis on the same point when she says: " The majority of the higher classes are getting Western secular education, which is undermining their faith in their ancestral religion. They are not getting anything better to take the place of the old religion in their hearts, and are, therefore, without God, without hope, without Christ, going down socially and morally, and becoming very irreligious."

In all these countries, therefore, the spread of secular education, with all the good that it is doing, has an aspect that is dangerous. Being devoid of all religious character, it inevitably gives the false impression that religion is not a necessary part of life, and when men find that the old religions cannot stand the light of criticism, they naturally are content to have no religion at all. This is what is happening to-day on a large scale.

Even as regards the many who are being driven by their new learning, not to close their minds against religion, but to search earnestly for a new religion more adequate than the old, there is a disquieting element in the present situation. The transition to Christianity is not so natural now as it was formerly. The non-Christian religions are recognizing their own inadequacy, are accordingly attempting to adapt themselves to the new conditions, and are manifesting increased activity, enterprise, and aggressiveness. Efforts are being put forth to regain and strengthen their influence over classes which have been slipping from their grasp and to extend their sway over peoples who have hitherto not been reached by them. These efforts are, unfortunately, succeeding to a great degree, and many are being thus kept away from Christianity who were open to receive it.

The revival of Buddhism is particularly noticeable in Japan, Burma, and Ceylon. Temples and shrines have been renovated in some districts, and the priests are manifesting greater activity. Most interesting is the semi-Christian modification of the methods and practices and to some extent the ideas of Buddhism. There are regular preaching-places where Buddhist preachers now expound their doctrines. The number of Buddhist schools and colleges is multiplying, especially in Ceylon and Burma. A large Buddhist college has been planned for Tokyo. Young Men's Buddhist Associations, Young Women's Buddhist Associations, and Buddhist Guilds have sprung up here and there. Special work has been inaugurated on behalf of children, such as Sunday schools, catechism classes, and religious instruction in day schools. Some Buddhist orphanages have been established to prevent destitute children from seeking admission into Christian institutions. The press is also being largely used. Manuals of instruction, tracts, pamphlets, and books are circulated in large numbers. Better training is being afforded the priests, especially in Japan. A large Buddhist theological school has been established in Kyoto, and young men are flocking there from all quarters. The most energetic workers, as well as the most generous givers, are the laymen. The most notable fact, however, is that Buddhism is seeking, not only to defend itself but also to take the offensive or aggressive attitude.

The Japanese Buddhists have organized a missionary society and have sent workers even to the mainland of Asia. The Jodo Sect are engaging in an evangelistic movement in Japan to commemorate the seven hundredth anniversary of the founding of their sect. In Burma the Buddhists are being reinforced by many converts from among the hill tribes. It is reported also that among the adherents of Buddhism in Ceylon and Burma are several Europeans. A general Buddhist society in Rangoon is raising funds for the translation of the Pali Buddhist scriptures into English, for spreading Buddhism in London, and for bringing out from England a number of Englishmen to enter the Buddhist priesthood. The southern part of the island of Ceylon is Buddhist, and while Buddhism there, until about the year 1880, was comparatively inert, it has since then been largely resuscitated. Its leaders carry on an aggressive propaganda. They imitate Christian phraseology, speaking, for example, of " our Lord and Saviour Buddha," and they also observe Buddha's birthday. Yet, in spite of all the activity, the introduction of new and improved methods, and the development of the spirit of propagandism, there is apparently little serious effort made to purify Buddhism of its corruptions. Rather they are condoned and explained away.

The movement is, moreover, decidedly more hostile to Christianity than it has been in the past, representing Christianity as alien and Buddhism as national. This attempt to identify Buddhism with national patriotism and to urge upon people that loyalty to the country implies loyalty to this religion is undoubtedly one of the most serious and significant aspects of the Buddhist revival.

Attention should be called to many new sects which are springing up in Japan and China. In Japan in recent years a new religion called Tenrikyo has come into vogue. It is neither avowedly Buddhist nor apparently idolatrous. There seems to be something attractive about it to the common people, for it is claimed that it already has between three and four millions of adherents. It has grown so rapidly that lately official recognition has been accorded to it by the Government. The growth of these sects is a sign of the unrest among the people and of their religious longings.

There is a very resolute effort being made by many of the most influential men in China to exalt Confucianism with its excellent ethical system above Christianity, which is belittled as a foreign religion. A comparatively recent edict raised Confucius to the rank of deity. Hitherto the worship of Confucius has been regarded as paying respect to the teacher *par excellence*—the Sage of China, but he is now exalted to equal rank with Heaven, possibly in order to give him a place corresponding to that of Jesus Christ in the worship of the West. This is significant, not as indicative of an increasing influence exerted by Confucius, but rather of a desire to conserve the influence manifestly waning, as modern learning discloses his superstitions and ignorance of fundamental facts. According to imperial edict, divine honors are to be offered to him by officials and by government students. Without this adoration of Confucius young men are not permitted to study in schools recognized by the Government, and are excluded from holding government offices. Those working on behalf of the educated classes find that their principal obstacle is this obligatory adoration of Confucius and the disabilities suffered by those who do not comply with the requirement. In a country like China exclusion from the official classes is regarded as a very serious matter, and until this obstacle is removed, missionary effort on behalf of the educated classes will be carried on under a serious handicap. The writings of Confucius have been translated by an educated Chinese into such idiomatic English that they are attracting the attention of students and scholars as never before. The government schools are also actively promoting the study and observance of the teachings of Confucius. The Rev. G. H. Bondfield writes: " Without question attempts will be made to reconstruct Chinese thought on the basis of Confucian teaching, with a little Western science and religion thrown in."

Hinduism is manifesting increased antagonism to Christianity. In different parts of India there is a revival of orthodox Hinduism as contrasted with the Neo-Hindu propaganda. This doubtless means more opposition, and yet it indicates, too, that the people are getting alarmed, and testifies to the progress which its opponents see that Christianity is making. In this light the revival of Hinduism is inevitable and desirable. It will in the end only hasten the progress of Christianity, as did the revival of paganism in the Roman Empire. Wherever there is strong opposition it is a sign that the minds of the people are occupied with the subject, and this enlarges the opportunity for Christian work. The Hindus, like the Buddhists, have been quick to learn Christian methods of religious propaganda, and they are meeting the Christian methods by imitating them in the interests of their own faith. They send out street preachers who give themselves largely to opposing Christianity, rather than to promulgating Hindu doctrines. They have a tract society, and issue many publications. They have Young Men's Hindu Associations and various other organizations formed after the pattern of Christian activities. That they have become alarmed by the inroads of Christianity is seen from the following extract taken from a pamphlet issued by the Hindu Tract Society and designed to arouse Hindus to sharper opposition: " Do you not know that the number of the Christians is increasing and the number of Hindu religionists decreasing every day? How long will water remain in a reservoir which continually lets out but receives none in? Let all the people join as one man to banish Christianity from our land." One of the best indications of the new spirit of the Hindus is the aggressive efforts which they are putting forth to in-

A HINDU FESTIVAL ON THE GANGES

fluence the outcastes. They are trying to raise the downtrodden classes and to give to them a certain definite standing in the Hindu community. Among the Namasudras, a tribe in Eastern Bengal two million strong, a social ferment is in progress and the Hindus as well as the workers of other religions are hoping for large accessions from the movement. The Santals, a large aboriginal tribe, are also in a state of transition, and are especially influenced by the Hindus. It is said that they are adopting the worst elements of Hindu life and religion; the lower form of Hinduism, with the worship of Durga, Kali, and Siva, with its sensuality and dishonesty, is creeping in. The Hindus are also seeking to influence the aboriginal tribes in the hill districts, and there is danger that the Sikhs may lapse into Hinduism. It is a further interesting and striking fact, that even as far away as the Fiji Islands, the Hindus, who are working on the plantations, are bringing an assimilating influence to bear upon the aboriginal inhabitants.

The ferment which Christianity has created among the educated classes of India is apparent even on the surface, but one of the most marked tendencies may be discerned in those schools of Neo-Hinduism which have developed during the past few decades. The most important of these are the Arya Somaj, chiefly in the Punjab and the United Provinces; the Brahmo Somaj, in Bengal; the Theosophists, principally in Southern India; and the Radha Swamis, in Northern India. They differ in many respects, but they are alike in that they have all been influenced by Chris-

tianity and have adopted many Christian expressions
and methods, and that they all magnify certain points
of Hinduism. Chief among these movements in point
of activity and influence is the Arya Somaj. While its
leaders may condemn the practices of Hinduism and
may adc t many of the principles and teachings and
methods of Christianity, they still remain within the
pale of Hinduism and earnestly oppose the Christian
movement. This movement has grown rapidly and has
schools and colleges, missionaries and societies. They
advocate the education of women, reject idolatry, and
seek to reduce the number of castes. Though re-
morseless in their antagonism to Christianity, they
mark a distinct advance upon popular Hinduism, and,
in the judgment of many missionaries, are preparing
the way of the Lord. The Rev. W. E. S. Holland, the
leader of the Oxford and Cambridge Hostel at Allaha-
bad, expresses this well: " The ideas which the Arya
Somaj raises without ability to satisfy them, and the
manifest contradictions of its system, mean a not remote collapse into the arms of Christianity."

The Rev. Herbert Anderson, however, in writing
regarding these efforts to revive or adapt the Indian
religions, gives expression to the opposite point of
view when he says: " There is no greater danger to the
success of our enterprise than the desire of the leaders
of non-Christian faiths to assimilate Christian truth
and claim Christ for their own systems—an addition
that can be made without radically altering the creed
or conduct of those who accept Him." They are just
now putting forth great efforts to influence the low

caste people. They do not really give them any new religion, but they fill their minds with prejudices against the foreigners, and strive on patriotic grounds to keep the people in subjection to Hinduism. If they succeed in convincing these outcaste portions of the population that they may hope for recognition from the Hindus, the attraction of Hinduism will be too strong for them to resist, and the door of Christian opportunity will close.

Of all the non-Christian religions, Mohammedanism exhibits the greatest solidarity and the most activity and aggressiveness, and is conducting a more widespread propaganda at the present time than any other religion save Christianity. In the Turkish Empire there has recently been a recrudescence of Moslem fanaticism. The forces that brought about the reactionary events of the spring of 1909, and that were responsible for the Cilician massacres were grouped under a so-called Mohammedan League. This league is intensely antagonistic to the spread of the Gospel among the Moslems, and under it the bigoted are becoming more bigoted. It was intended by Abdul Hamid to intensify Moslem fanaticism and hatred of Christians, and its members, though now in hiding, form the body of the old orthodox party who look down with scorn upon all other sects. Islam is linking itself with the atheism and deism of Western lands, and is securing much protection and also added prestige by the support it receives at the hands of officials from the West who have broken with Christianity. These men carry over to the Moslem camp all the armory of the deistic and atheistic schools.

In India, the country having the largest Mohammedan population, there is a renaissance of Islam. The power of the Prophet is still great, and Islam is ready to receive and seal perpetually, as her own, Hindus of low caste who lose faith in their own religion or seek to better their condition. They are pushing their propaganda, sending out preachers and working hard to convert the low caste and outcaste people. In some parts of the country large bodies of these depressed classes and also numbers of the hill tribes have gone over to Islam. Their advance in India is proved by an increase in the Mohammedan population in India of about six millions in the ten years preceding the last census. Dr. J. C. R. Ewing of Lahore expresses the belief that unless the Church avails itself of the marvelous opportunity now presented by the tens of millions of low caste people, within the next ten years the bulk of those who have not been given a status in relation to the Hindus, will have become Mohammedan. While there is no serious danger that China will become a Moslem state, Mohammedanism is there also manifesting fresh interest and vigor. By correspondence the mullahs are kept in touch with the political and religious movements of the world of Islam, and by the visits of Moslem missionaries from Arabia and elsewhere, efforts are constantly made to revive the faith. Moreover, in other parts of China, in Chihli, for example, there are similar indications of activity.

The Moslems of Russia are showing great zeal. There are indications that the Pan-Islamic movement has reached Bokhara and Kabul, as well as Orenburg and Tiflis. Not only is there discussion of social reform in the Moslem press of Russia, but the Tartar paper, *Terjuman*, recently contained a proposition calling for a Pan-Islamic Congress to discuss the reformation of Islam.

In the East Indies, Islam, which for a long time was but a mere veneer, is daily becoming a more pervasive and dominant faith. It is advancing rapidly and persistently, absorbing step by step the existing remnants of heathenism. Greatly increased travel to Mecca, brought about by better means of communication and lower rates, is establishing Mohammedanism among the Malays. The returned pilgrims become henceforth ardent defenders and propagators of the faith. In Sumatra, Islam is advancing into hitherto pagan territories, and unless the Church promptly does more to meet the desire for education and enlightenment, there is danger that the population will more and more accept Mohammedanism. In Java, Mohammedanism shows new life in the establishment of a Moslem university, and in the production of an edition of the Koran in Javanese. The intercourse between Java and Mecca is extremely active, thousands of Javanese annually making the pilgrimage. The number of teachers of the Koran is multiplying greatly. Not less than 20,000 Arabs are carrying on an effective and profitable propaganda in the East Indies as teachers of Islam. The inhabitants are coming more and more under the influ-

ence of Mohammedanism, and are thus being made
less accessible to the work of the Dutch missionaries.
The same great movement is in process in Celebes, New
Guinea, the Philippines, and other islands and groups
of islands.

Two forces are contending for Africa—Christianity
and Mohammedanism. In many respects the more
aggressive is Mohammedanism. It dominates Africa
on its western half as far south as 10° N. lati-
tude, and on its eastern half, as far south as 5° N.;
and it is ever pushing its conquests beyond its own territory, not only down the East Coast but also into the
interior and to the tribes on the West Coast. If things
continue as they are now tending, Africa may become
a Mohammedan continent. Mohammedanism comes
to the African people as a higher religion than their
own, with the dignity of an apparently higher civilization and of world power. It is rapidly received by
these eager listeners. Once received, it is Christianity's
most formidable enemy. It permits a laxity of morals,
in some cases worse than that of heathendom. It sanc-
tions polygamy. It breeds pride and arrogance, and
thus hardens the heart against the Word of God. It
is spread by those who do not differ essentially from
the natives in their ideas and customs, whereas
Christianity, until a force of native workers can be
prepared, must be spread by Europeans who differ
greatly from the natives.

The absorption of native races into Islam is proceed-
ing rapidly and continuously in practically all parts of
the continent. Convincing evidence of this fact has

been presented by missionaries along the Nile, in East Central Africa, in Southeast Africa, on different parts of the West Coast, in Northern Nigeria, in the Sudan, in different parts of the Congo Basin, in parts lying south of the Congo, and even in South Africa. Mohammedan traders are finding their way into the remotest parts of the continent, and it is well known that every Mohammedan trader is more or less a Mohammedan missionary. Wherever a Mohammedan penetrates, he makes converts to Islam. Paganism is doomed. As has been said above, animistic faiths crumble quickly before any higher and more dogmatic religion. Either Christianity or Islam will prevail throughout Africa, and Islam is pushing hard to win the pagan states and peoples.

This remarkable and widespread activity in all the non-Christian religions is the direct counterpart of the activity in the political sphere. It is due to the growth of the conviction that if the old faiths are to hold the place which they have hitherto held in the allegiance of their adherents, they must bestir themselves and adopt new methods. It is being freely recognized further, that Christianity has many advantages which enable it to meet with greater confidence and effectiveness the influence of modern education, and an effort is being made almost everywhere—even within Mohammedanism—to adopt certain features of Christianity which, when added to the other religions, will, it is hoped, give to them the same power. This readiness to alter is itself a confession of weakness and may well be read as a prophecy of the complete surrender to Christian truth. All of them, in spite of their bitter opposition to it, are being made to feel the power of Christianity, and what modifications have been introduced are a tacit recognition of the superiority with which Christianity is endowed.

None of the movements which we have been considering can be contemplated by the Church with a quiet mind, for each of them contains a menace to Christian progress. Moreover, who is to blame for the evil influences that go out from our Christian lands, if it be not the Church of Christ? What it has failed to do in the past it should seek to do now. There are still great regions and countless communities to which the vices and diseases of corrupt civilization have not yet spread, and unmistakably it is the will of God that the missionary movement be extended promptly and far more aggressively and widely that Christianity may give the people strength to stand against the temptations that are certain to attack them. The large plans for the extension of railway systems in different parts of Asia and Africa accentuate the urgency of the situation, because the advent of railways will bring an influx of ungodly men who will quickly make the task of evangelization much more difficult. In this respect the present is an opportunity which will soon pass away. Every year will bring new and powerful counter attractions within easy reach of the natives. It is much easier to bring the Gospel to bear on a heathen in his natural state than upon the man who has become familiar with the worst side of the so-called Christian civilization.

Equally it is the duty of the Church to make a supreme effort to Christianize more largely the impact of Christendom upon the non-Christian world. To this end more adequate efforts are required not only to surround the representatives of our commerce and industries with strong Christian influences as they go forth to reside in distant port cities, but also to make sure that the principles and spirit of Jesus Christ dominate all our social, commercial, political, and international relations with the peoples and governments of non-Christian nations. The missionary forces cannot win the non-Christian world for Christ until Christian nations and all their influences are more thoroughly permeated with the spirit of Christ.

As regards the advance of education the duty of the Church is, if possible, still greater. The development of moral and religious education is rightly held to be one of the most pressing problems in the West. This is in spite of the facts that we already have the assistance of the Christian Church and the Christian home and of much organized Christian work for students, that the great bulk of our teachers are professing Christians and many of them active Christian workers, that our literature is penetrated with the Christian spirit and our whole civilization founded on Christian presuppositions. None of these aids are present in the East, except as they have been supplied by the meagre force of missionaries. The scientific and utilitarian side of our education is far more easily appreciated by the Oriental at the present time than its moral and idealistic side.

The scientific temper, as he catches it, is apt to shear him at the same time of his superstition and his reverence. The scientific explanation of the universe is so precise and perfect as compared with his grandmother's myths, that he cannot see its limitations, moreover, it fits in well with his bent towards fatalism and unspirituality. If, therefore, moral education is a need in the West, what word can we find to express its absolute indispensableness for the East? The only way to prevent education from producing agnosticism and materialism is to give education of a Christian character. The Christian Church cannot permit these vast masses who are eagerly demanding Western learning thus to be turned against itself. Rather is it a duty to realize the present as a call and a special opportunity for advancing Christ's Kingdom. The difficulty which the Chinese Government is experiencing in securing a sufficient number of competent teachers is common also to other lands and affords a great opening to Christian schools and colleges. There should be a great expansion of Christian educational missions. It is Western education that the Chinese are clamoring for, and will have. If the Church can give it to them, plus Christianity, they will take it; otherwise they will get it elsewhere, without Christianity—and that speedily. If in addition to direct evangelistic and philanthropic work in China, the Church can in the next decade train several thousands of Christian teachers, it will be in a position to meet this unparalleled opportunity. In India, too, the crisis calls for a greatly increased number of efficient mission schools

ANCIENT EXAMINATION HALLS, NANKING

This system is now supplanted by modern educational institutions throughout China

and colleges, manned with thoroughly qualified and earnest Christian teachers, and conducted so far as possible on the residential plan, with the view to giving the Spirit of God as carefully prepared an opportunity as possible. The unrest of the educated classes calls not only for a strengthening of the missionary institutions, especially in the direction of making their Christian influence more effective, but also for a multiplication at student centers of wisely planned efforts directed to influence those of the educated class after leaving college as well as the students now in non-missionary colleges. If Christians do not rise to the occasion, educated Hindus and Mohammedans will take things into their own hands and will establish educational and philanthropic institutions to be carried on under non-Christian management.

The renewed activity of the non-Christian religions further emphasizes the duty of the Church at this time. Some missionary statesmen believe that Africa (because of the ease with which the pagan religions yield to the first attacks of any higher faith) for the present has a pre-eminent claim on the attention and resources of those missionary societies which are related to the regions in which Moslem advance is imminent. The aboriginal population and the outcastes of India, as well as animists in other regions, likewise present an urgent claim. If Christian work for these depressed classes could soon be multiplied many fold, multitudes of people would embrace Christianity within a generation. Unless the advance which non-Christian religions are making is met and counteracted, the Christian missionary enterprise will be increasingly handicapped. Mohammedanism and Hinduism are both competing with Christianity for the adherence of many peoples. Surely with such a crisis impending, it is the duty of the Church, as it is the call of God, to renew its energies and whole-heartedly to advance.

THE RISING SPIRITUAL TIDE IN THE NON-CHRISTIAN WORLD

CHAPTER III

THE RISING SPIRITUAL TIDE IN THE NON-CHRISTIAN WORLD

WHEN the conditions throughout the non-Christian world inviting a comprehensive advance are considered, as well as the serious obstacles and critical tendencies which threaten the progress of Christianity, both the urgency and the difficulty of the task seem overwhelming, if not depressing; but a survey of recent triumphs and of the present-day working of the Christian forces in non-Christian lands, affords abundant ground for hopefulness and confidence. In the great battle of Moukden, with a frontage of many miles, a certain regiment or division of the Japanese army, hard pressed at times by the enemy, might have feared that defeat was impending; but the general in charge of the Japanese operations, in touch with the whole line by means of wireless telegraphy and other appliances of the modern signaling corps, knew well that, taking the battle as a whole, victory was assured. So on the world-wide battlefield of Christianity, while there are apparent discouragements in some parts of the field, and while certain divisions of the Christian forces are being hard pressed by the forces that oppose, taking the world as a whole, victory is assured if the present campaign be adequately supported and pressed.

It seems incredible that within the lifetime of many now living there were placed in different parts of Japan edict boards on which were official announcements offering rewards for the apprehension of persons found either professing or propagating the Christian faith. In contrast, one finds to-day a Japanese Protestant Christian community numbering fully 70,000 communicants. In addition, the Eastern or Greek Church numbers 30,000, and the members of the Roman Catholic Church number 60,000. If the number of adherents be taken into account the number of Christians connected with these three great sections of the Christian Church must considerably exceed one-quarter of a million. There has been an increase of seventy per cent. in the number of Protestant Church members during the last decade. Moreover, Christianity in Japan began with the Samurai or knightly class, so that its influence is a hundredfold greater than its statistical strength. When the best educated men of the nation speak regarding the religions of the country, Buddhism and Christianity, if they discriminate in favor of either religion it is always in favor of Christianity, because of its high character and transforming influence, although the number of adherents of Buddhism reaches into tens of millions, while the number of adherents of Christianity includes only tens of thousands. In the present Japanese Parliament twelve members of three hundred and eighty are Christians, or nearly twice as many as in the last Parliament. An investigation has shown that the ratio of Christians to the total number of students in the

THE HARBOR OF OSAKA

higher institutions of the great government school system of Japan is over thirty times as great as the proportion of Christian young men to the total number of young men in the country, and this ratio has steadily increased during the present generation. Facts like these show that Christianity has won a place of great and growing influence among the educated and influential classes of the nation. A further illustration was the gift by the Emperor of $5000 toward the work carried on by the Young Men's Christian Association on behalf of the soldiers in the recent war.

In the recent past, several of the Christian bodies at work in Japan have had encouraging results in conversions. In some parts of the country there have been revivals; notable among these was the Taikyo Dendo, a spiritual awakening which swept through the Japanese Islands a few years ago, and was promoted by the united efforts of practically all of the Christian workers in the country. Under its influence thousands of people were converted. Still more recently there have been conducted the so-called concentration evangelistic campaigns, waged largely by the Japanese workers themselves. One of the best examples of these is the revival which has taken place during the present year, 1910, in the commercial metropolis, Osaka. Workers representing forty-two churches and preaching-places united, and 104 speakers participated. Each of the large mass meetings was attended by over 2000, and the church services throughout the city were crowded, day after day. Over 1300 persons registered as inquirers or as applicants for baptism, a number equal to one-third of the total church membership of the city. On one Sunday in March, 1910, 355 of the converts were baptized in connection with the churches of one communion alone. This awakening is directly traceable to united intercession, and to loyal and unselfish co-operative effort on the part of all the workers of the different churches.

The Christian work carried on among the 750,000 Japanese soldiers in Manchuria by the Young Men's Christian Association movement, was one of the most successful efforts of its kind ever conducted in any country. In accordance with the desire of the War Department of the Japanese Government, this movement was regarded as the exponent of all the Christian forces of Japan, and was accorded permission to minister to the comfort of the soldiers. All through the campaign the Government granted special privileges to those engaged in this service. The work was placed in charge of experienced secretaries, both Japanese and foreign, and some of the missions also allocated able missionaries to co-operate. Assistance was rendered the soldiers both before leaving Japan and after they reached the seat of war, as well as on the transports, but the principal service was performed in Manchuria. There buildings and tents were secured which were constantly thronged with soldiers who came to avail themselves of the various privileges afforded by the Association. Opportunities were offered for reading Japanese papers and other literature, stereopticon exhibitions were given, facilities for correspondence were afforded, and millions of letters and post-cards were written and posted by the soldiers, who thereby conveyed to the people in countless cities and villages in Japan the information as to the service which a Christian organization was rendering them. Day by day, not only in these buildings and tents, but also on the railway trains and in the hospitals, evangelistic addresses and appeals were made to the throngs of soldiers, who, solemnized by the impending dangers, were peculiarly responsive to messages concerning the religious life. Missionaries have said that in this campaign the Gospel was preached with fulness and power by the few scores of workers to more of the aggressive classes of Japanese men than were reached during the same period by the hundreds of missionaries working in Japan itself. With the co-operation of the Bible Societies the Gospels were widely circulated among the troops. Although accurate statistics have not been gathered, large numbers of men were converted as a result of the efforts put forth on their behalf. The attitude of many officers was changed from one of hostility or indifference to that of outspoken sympathy. Since the war it has been found that the practical helpfulness of this campaign and of the ministration of Christian workers in hospitals, has served to commend the cause of Christianity to the families and friends of many of the soldiers, and to open doors for Christian effort and influence in all parts of Japan.

The evangelistic mission carried on by the Christian Student Movement of Japan in connection with the Conference of the World's Student Christian Federation, held in Tokyo in 1907, was also a remarkably fruitful spiritual effort. During the three weeks this mission was in progress the claims of Christ were presented to tens of thousands of government students and schoolboys in all the student communities of Japan, resulting in three thousand becoming Christian inquirers. Christianity is making great advance, not only among the educated and influential classes of the country but also among those at the other end of the social scale. This is well illustrated by the account of the recent revival in the Tokachi Prison, in the Hokkaido, as given in an illustrated pamphlet entitled, " How the Holy Spirit came to the Hokkaido, Japan." It is a thrilling story of a modern Pentecost.

To such facts should be added, what some regard as the most striking evidence of the work and power of God in Japan—the spread of Christian teachings and ideals and their influence upon social life and practices. This is revealed in the movement led by Christians which resulted in releasing thousands of the inmates of the brothels, in the effective temperance crusade, and in the establishment of many benevolent institutions, such as the famous Ishii orphanages. A very general dissatisfaction with the old religions exists throughout the land. Shintoism is no longer classified as a religion by the Government, but merely as a patriotic association for preserving the memory of ancestors. Notwithstanding what has been stated regarding the revival of Buddhism in certain sections, the fact remains that in parts of Japan it is losing its hold on its adherents. There are many and multiplying instances where the people have abolished idols and forsaken the temples, although they may not yet have accepted some other religion as a substitute. In the cities Buddhism has far less influence, even with the illiterate classes, than it has in the rural districts. It has little power over the people, and ethically and religiously its recent influence has not contributed to the higher life of Japan or China. There are few educated men who profess belief in Buddhism as a regulative, transforming, and energizing influence in their lives. They are realizing that it is lacking in both spiritual and moral power. So much is this the case that an endeavor has been made in the schools to give moral education apart altogether from religion, but the failure of this also is being recognized. The late Mr. Fukuzawa, a leader of thought in Japan, though himself an agnostic, said, before his death, that he had felt it " a great loss that he had lived his life without religion, and that he would recommend Christianity to his friends without any hesitation," and it is said that to-day " there is among the leaders of the nation a large party composed of men who are thoroughly dissatisfied with the present outlook, even alarmed at it; and, though not themselves necessarily Christians, would gladly see their country adopt the faith." The spread of this conviction, that Christianity alone can provide an adequate basis for individual and national life, is surely preparing the way for a general acceptance of Christianity throughout Japan and for giving it a position of large influence.

On Christmas Day, 1887, three years after the first missionaries entered Korea, seven baptized Christians in Seoul united behind closed doors in the first celebration of the Holy Communion. To-day that interesting land is wide open to the Christian Gospel. There are now, including those under instruction for church membership, fully 200,000 Koreans who acknowledge Jesus Christ as Lord, and the number is increasing at the rate of over 30 per cent. each year. The visitor to Korea is impressed by the fact that the Spirit of God is working with great power in all parts of the country. People of all classes are being brought under the sway of Christ. The eagerness manifested among the Korean people to learn of Christ is so great that the missionaries everywhere are overwhelmed in their attempts to meet the flood-tide of opportunity pressing upon them, and have little time to go after the people or to do pioneer work.

The Koreans are Bible-studying Christians. The Bible is the book having the largest sale among them; it has been disseminated even among the remotest villages. Fully one-sixth of the entire church membership are enrolled in Bible training-classes or conferences which are held from time to time at principal mission centers, and continue from a few days to three weeks. It is no uncommon thing for the Christians to make a ten days' journey to attend one of these gatherings for Bible study. The Koreans are praying Christians. At Phyengyang, in connection with one church, the midweek prayer-meeting has had for years an average attendance of 1100, and is possibly the largest meeting for united intercession which assembles anywhere in the world.

The Korean Christians are also Christians who give liberally of their substance. Eighty per cent. of the work of the Korean Church is already self-supporting. Hundreds of Korean leaders and lay preachers serve without receiving any remuneration. Dr. George Heber Jones reports that, " Korean men have been known to mortgage their houses that mortgages might be removed from the houses of God; to sell their crops of good rice, intended for family consumption, purchasing inferior millet to live upon through the winter, and giving the difference in cost for the support of workers to preach among their own countrymen. Korean women have given their wedding rings, and even cut off their hair that it might be sold and the amount devoted to the spread of the Gospel."

The Korean Christians are also working Christians. Thousands of them last year gave from one week to one month each to the work of proclaiming the Gospel in neighboring and in distant communities. It is probable that a larger proportion of Korean Christians have won others to Christ than of those in the Church of any other land. Often the test question in connection with admission to church membership is, " Have you led some other soul to Jesus Christ?" The Korean Church is a missionary Church; its members are working among the Korean colonies in Hawaii, on the Pacific Coast of the United States, in Mexico, as well as in Manchuria and Siberia. A missionary tells of a Korean who reported that he had heard that, in a certain Manchurian city, there were 100,000 Koreans, that there were many brigands there, that the rice was not good to eat, but that he wished to go there to preach the Gospel, and as he had three sons he thought that, growing up among the Chinese, they would learn the Chinese language so well that they would become missionaries to the Chinese. It is this spirit which explains the rapid development and extension of the Korean Church. There is every prospect that if the Church of the West presses forward its missionary efforts, Korea will be the first non-Christian nation to become Christianized in the modern missionary era. The Honorable T. H. Yun, the most influential Christian of Korea, voices his conviction that, " The next ten years will tell more for the evangelization of Korea than the fifty years thereafter." The thorough evangelization of one nation actually accomplished would serve as a practical object-lesson to the whole Church, and would inspire Christians in all other non-Christian nations.

In China, the promise is greater to-day than at any time in the past. When Protestant missionaries first went to China, so unfruitful did the soil appear, that one hundred years ago Dr. Milne, Robert Morrison's first colleague, predicted that in a century there would be 1000 communicants and adherents to Protestant Christianity in China. At the end of the first thirty-five years of the missionary history of China, it seemed as though Dr. Milne's prophecy might not be fulfilled, for there were but six converts to Christianity. Even twenty years later, when Bishop Moule of Mid-China first went out, there were, according to his statement, only fifty Protestant Christian communicants. Since then, however, the tide has begun to flow, and in the year 1896 there were as many as 80,000 communicants. Now there are fully 175,000, and were the number of Protestant adherents included, the number would be nearly half a million. This rapid increase is being continued to-day. Contrary to the general impression, the greatest advances of Christianity have been made since the Boxer uprising.

Reports tell of spiritual awakenings in widely separated parts of China—west, south, north, and central. As an example, the revival in Hinghua, in the Fukien Province, may be mentioned. This awakening began a few months ago and seems to be still in the initial stages; the meetings day after day are crowding the large tabernacle with audiences numbering about five thousand. Dr. William Brewster, in writing of this revival, says, " No language can describe the power of God as here manifested. There was no hysteria, no prostration, but simply conviction of sin and confession, restitution, forsaking sin, accepting Christ as Saviour by thousands, and going out anointed for witnessing to His power to save." Evangelistic campaigns conducted by the late Dr. Lee, the eminent Chinese evangelist, in different parts of the country, were also occasions of the mighty working of the living God. The Rev. J. Goforth of the Canadian Presbyterian Mission has had remarkable success in conducting thirty special missions in six different provinces. He testifies that in every place he has seen God's glorious power manifested. In some cases those who attended these special missions carried the evangelistic spirit to other communities.

One of the most wonderful revivals of modern times is the one among the degraded and illiterate tribes in Southwest China. The movement has extended most widely among the Miao, a vigorous, aboriginal race, including about seventy tribes, which have maintained a state of semi-independence of the Chinese Government. This revival has been going on steadily for over seven years; during that time many villages have become wholly Christian, and in hundreds of other villages Christian bands are witnessing for Christ. Many men who were once drunkards are now sober, and women who formerly were leading immoral lives are now leading victorious lives under the power of Christ. It is estimated that over 20,000 of these tribesmen have broken with heathenism and turned to Christ, largely as a result of the efforts of those who had themselves been converted but recently from heathenism. Mr. J. R. Adam of the China Inland Mission, in describing a tour which he made within the past two years in the Miao country, tells of the large numbers who came to hear the preaching of the Gospel. On one Sunday literally thousands were present at the morning service, and nine hundred celebrated the Holy Communion. In all the villages he visited, he was kept busy examining and baptizing converts. Surprisingly few cases of discipline were brought to his attention. As in the case of the Welsh revival, singing has been a prominent feature of

this movement among the Miao. The central message
of the revival has been the refrain—

> There is a fountain filled with blood
> Drawn from Emmanuel's veins;
> And sinners plunged beneath that flood,
> Lose all their guilty stains.

The thirst among the Chinese for knowledge concerning Christianity is remarkable. Dr. Griffith John
has said that when he reached China it was difficult
even to give away copies of the New Testament, and
that this had to be done in secret. Two years ago, the
Tract Society in his region sold a million and a half
copies of different pieces of Christian literature, and
the Presbyterian Press in Shanghai during the same
year disposed of one million six hundred thousand
copies. The Bible Societies of Britain and America
have had a similar encouraging expansion of their
work.

The Christward movement in China is making quite
as great progress among the students as among the
masses. Ten years ago, it was impossible to obtain
access to the *literati* or government students. Within
the past three or four years the largest halls which
could be obtained in several of the principal student
centers of China would not hold the crowds of modern
government students who thronged the evangelistic
meetings conducted under the auspices of the Student
Christian Association movement. This has occurred
in connection with missions conducted by several different missionaries and visiting Christian workers

from abroad. These meetings, which often lasted
three hours, have almost without exception been attended with large results in the definite conversion of
students; and there have been similar encouragements
in connection with the campaign waged among the
thousands of Chinese students in Tokyo, under the
auspices of the Young Men's Christian Association.
No month passes in which some of these students do
not make open confession and become baptized.

The Chinese Christians in different parts of the
country and of all social classes are assuming as never
before the burden of responsibility for the propagation
of the Gospel. There are gratifying evidences of this
among the converts of the peasant and merchant
classes, but the most striking examples are those afforded by the colleges and schools.

The activities of a Christian Association in a college
in Swatow may serve to illustrate the sense of responsibility as accepted by the Christian students in all
parts of China. The institution has in all only twenty
students, but every one of these is enrolled in Bible
classes. In addition to their Christian work in the college they are conducting a night school three evenings
in the week for the people of the village. Every student in the institution is engaged in evangelistic work
in places near the school. They send representatives
to the railway station to sell Christian literature, and
on festival days, when there are unusual crowds, they
travel on the trains for this purpose. Three miles
from the school there is a town of ten thousand people,
among whom there is not a Christian, and there the

BIRTHPLACE OF THE STUDENT VOLUNTEER MOVEMENT, MOUNT HERMON, MASS.

Student Association has rented and furnished a house
in which they conduct evangelistic services regularly.
The Student Associations of no country are doing more
widespread and thorough work among people outside
of the colleges than are those in China. Moreover,
they are raising up large numbers of Christian workers.
In the Peking University there is a Volunteer Band
composed of over two hundred students who have
dedicated their lives to Christian service, although this
involved turning their backs upon opportunities of receiving far larger salaries in commercial pursuits or in
government service. A few months ago, after a revival in the Union Christian College in the Shantung
Province, 104 of the College students and twenty-eight
of the boys in the High School consecrated their lives
to Christian work.

The indirect influences of Christianity in China are
becoming increasingly evident. As a result of the
example of medical missions, the Chinese are themselves devoting increasingly their gifts and their efforts
to the alleviation of physical suffering. The ablest and
most conspicuous leaders of the opium reform are
men who have come intimately in touch with Christianity. The crusade against foot-binding, while now
favored by an Imperial edict and taken up by officials
and gentry throughout the empire, was inaugurated
by Christians. The new government colleges are mod-
eled after the missionary institutions, an i all of them
close on Sunday. The new literature is so saturated
with ideals of liberty, justice, and social responsibility,
taken directly from Christian sources, that the Chinese

language has had to be materially altered to fit it to these new conceptions. The revision of the penal code which is now in progress means the abolition of torture and the adoption of Christian laws for the empire. Slavery, which was especially widespread among girls, has recently been prohibited by an edict of the Prince Regent, and women are rapidly being accorded the status which they enjoy in Christian lands. This latter fact is considered by many as the most significant reform now taking place in the country, and it is certainly one of the very clearest proofs of the growing influence which Christian ideals are having upon the life of China.

The entire history of missions in Manchuria has been characterized by genuine revivals. One of the most thoroughgoing and fruitful has been the spiritual awakening of the last two years. Beginning in Moukden, it soon spread to other centers, and everywhere with remarkable results. Dr. W. Phillips, of the Irish Presbyterian Mission, gives an account of one of these meetings which is typical. He says: " Deep conviction of sin has been the characteristic note of the revival. It has been so noticeable a feature that it has become almost a byword in the villages: ' Avoid these Christians. Their God is a Spirit of confessing, who will force you to disclose what no yamen could wring from you.' What the revival may lead to, no man can tell. The old religions have lost their hold on the people and the whole land is open to receive the Gospel. The spiritual fires are spreading from place to place and radiating their influence wider and wider; wherever

they come there is a ready response. Great signs and
wonders are still being wrought by the living God on
the Manchurian plains. Boxers who massacred Christians have been converted as a result of the spirit of
forgiveness shown by the injured Christians towards
their persecutors; whole towns have been moved by
the Spirit of God, and thousands added to the Church.
The whole of Manchuria seems to be stirred to its
depths."

Notwithstanding the unrest and disturbances in
India, the past few years have witnessed real progress
in the Christian propaganda. There have been large
ingatherings into the Kingdom of Christ. The awakening in the Welsh Mission in the Khasi Hills, leading to the conversion of thousands and to the quickening of the native Church, exerted an influence far
beyond that region. It did much to strengthen the
faith of the workers elsewhere, and to fire them with
the zeal of evangelism. The so-called " mass movements " in different parts of India are resulting each
year in turning a multitude of the outcastes and of the
members of the lower castes towards the Christian
fold. The readiness of these depressed masses to receive the Gospel and to accept baptism is indeed impressive. In the Telugu country thousands of vil-
lagers, including members of higher castes as well as
of depressed classes, are clamorously desiring to enter
the Church, while the available workers are not able
to meet the demand for religious teaching made upon
them. During a single year recently about three thousand souls in the southeast portion of the Nizam's

Dominions placed themselves under Christian instruction.

The characteristics and working of a mass movement may best be illustrated by a description of what took place in a Telugu village. The inhabitants, composed almost entirely of the depressed classes and outcastes, had become greatly dissatisfied with their state of degradation and with the general adverse conditions of their life. They had observed the social, economic, and intellectual changes and improvements in neighboring Christian communities where the people were formerly as degraded and depressed as themselves. They sent a deputation to the missionaries at a mission station some distance away and urged them to send a Christian teacher to the village, and indicated their willingness to place themselves under Christian instruction. Later, a catechist was sent, and he remained in their midst for nearly a year. During that time, he held services almost every day, and on many days both in the early morning and in the evening. He devoted himself to teaching them the facts about the life of Jesus Christ, and to expounding simply and clearly the fundamental Christian doctrines, observances, and customs. Under his positive instruction about Christianity, they discovered for themselves the low character of much of their religion, especially its debased idol worship, its devil dances, and other corrupt practices. The catechist called upon them to turn from their idols and to give up habits of drinking and immorality. In due time they tore down their temple and built a simple place for Christian worship. Such a radical step represented nothing less than a great revolution in their ideas and attitude. The giving up, on the part of many of them, of Sunday labor is also an impressive proof of the marked change, because most of the members of the community were very poor and dependent upon hard and constant work to provide for their needs. None were baptized until after several months of instruction and until after they had given satisfying evidence of a change of life as shown in repentance, in giving up sinful and questionable habits and associations, and in trust in Jesus as Saviour. When the catechist first came to this village, some ninety members of the community gathered round him under a tree at his first service. When he revisited the place there were 190 baptized Christians, eighty of whom were communicant members of the Church. He found eighty persons who could read the Bible, whereas at the time of the first visit none of them could do so. He bore testimony that the very expression of their countenances had been changed. Twelve confirmed drunkards had broken their evil habit and had paid debts which had hung over their families for over two generations. The whole community had been appreciably raised in its social and economic status. The change in disposition and character of many of the people had been so marked as to impress deeply the Brahman landlords, who at first opposed the coming of the catechist, and on one occasion had driven him out, but now begged him to visit other villages to carry on a similar work. They testified that the practice of stealing had been done away, and that the whole moral tone of the village had been changed. Some men who had been given to drink and had been in prison were found working for the temperance cause and seeking to convert their fellows. The Christians were giving liberally for the support and spread of the Gospel, some exhibiting great sacrifice. As a result of this genuine work of God in one village a similar spirit of dissatisfaction with their present conditions, and of desire for new and better things, had spread to neighboring villages. Men had not been greatly impressed by what Christianity might do for individuals, but the object lesson of a village community transformed by Christian teaching and the work of the Holy Spirit had served as a convincing evidence of the vitality and power of Christianity, and had led them to seek to bring its transforming influence to bear upon their corporate life.

Similar movements are reported in the United Provinces, in the Punjab, and in Western India. In one section of North India, at the present rate of ingathering, it will be only a few years until practically all of the " sweepers " will have come in; and there are at present signs of a break among a still larger class—the leather-workers. Several lower castes are very accessible. Bishop Warne, in writing about the mass movement in connection with the Methodist Episcopal Mission in the United Provinces, says, " I have now known this field for twenty years. This movement among the lower castes towards Christianity has taken place almost entirely during that period. The readiness to receive Gospel teaching and to accept baptism has been found wherever we have been able to extend our work with the needed vigor. This movement has already given us about 24,000 converts, and perhaps one-third of that number have died during these years." Some missions are baptizing as rapidly as they can thoroughly evangelize and teach. Others testify that they could double or quadruple the number of baptisms were they able to double their force of workers.

The missionaries in touch with these movements in India are alive to the perils involved, and they may be depended upon to safeguard the Church from serious mistakes. The opportunity is certainly great and urgent. The late Professor Satthianadhan of the Presidency College in Madras pointed out, in 1905, the hopeful aspect of the work of the Holy Spirit among the masses: " It is those very classes, depressed, trampled down, and looked upon as utterly incapable of improvement of any kind, that now, with the enlightening influence of Christianity, compete successfully with the highest castes and classes of Indian society in every direction. In my opinion, even if there had not been a single convert from the higher classes of Hindu society, the transformation which Christianity has wrought among the lower classes it has won over to its fold, is itself a clear evidence of its unique triumph in India."

The significance of the mass movement will be even better realized by pondering the following words of the Bishop of Madras: " The main fact which ought, I think, to determine the use we make of the forces at our disposal in India at the present day, is that there are 50,000,000 people in India who are quite ready to receive the Gospel message, to put themselves under Christian teaching and discipline, and to be baptized; and that, if a prompt, aggressive, and adequate campaign were carried on among them, it would be quite possible to gather something like 30,000,000 of them into the Christian Church during the next fifty years, to raise them morally, spiritually, and socially from the state of degradation and servitude in which Hinduism has kept them for the last two thousand years, and to furnish to the whole people of India, especially to the educated classes, a most powerful witness for the truth and power of the Christian faith."

These modern mass movements present an appeal to the Church to make a prompt and large advance. They will not be without their powerful influence on the higher castes and classes of India. May it not be that the Bishop of Madras is right in his contention that the future of India lies more with the pariah than with the Brahman? Be this as it may, the history of the Church shows that any great spiritual movement at the bottom of society sooner or later profoundly affects the upper strata.

It should be noted, however, that the movement toward Christ among the higher castes and educated classes of India also affords grounds for thanksgiving and hopefulness. There are among the higher castes, hundreds of people who, as a result of the impression made upon them by the transforming work of the Gospel among the low castes, and outcastes, as well as of direct efforts on their own behalf, have been led to give serious attention to Christianity, and in heart have come into sympathy with its teaching and spirit. Numbers of them have been baptized, and there is reason to believe that many more all over India are secret disciples and worshipers of Jesus Christ. A survey of the Indian Christian community will show that the number of converts from the higher castes, while not large, is increasing. A prominent worker among students in India has pointed out recently that there have been more conversions among the educated classes of India during the last ten years than in any previous decade in the history of Indian missions. The principal of one of the leading Christian colleges says that the student class was never so accessible to Christian influences as now. Missionaries and other observers in all sections of India emphasize the fact that comparatively few of the educated classes adhere to Hinduism in an unmodified form, and that not many of them have a vital faith in it as a personal religion. A leading Scottish missionary of many years' experience has said that nowadays no *bona fide* idolater is to be found among university men. The firm hold which the old religions and customs of India had upon the people is breaking down, and, as the Bishop of Lahore says, " There has been a gradual conversion of the attitude of the people toward Christianity." Christianity is coming more and more into its own in Hindustan, and the best thought of India is not toward Hinduism but toward Christ.

In all parts of the Turkish Empire and in Persia since the recent revolutions, there is a widespread spirit of inquiry, as shown by the unprecedented demand for the Scriptures. Mohammedanism has as strong a hold on its adherents as has any other non-Christian religion, but it is weakening in the case of the educated and better-informed men. The Koran and the newly proclaimed principles of liberty are not found to be suitable yoke-fellows. Notwithstanding the aggressive advance of Mohammedanism in some quarters of the world, as a religion it is making no marked intellectual or spiritual progress, and therefore it is not able to command the full allegiance of many of its adherents who are studying the modern learning.

The application of modern critical methods in India and elsewhere is serving to undermine faith in the Koran, so that it is no uncommon thing to find Moslems who concede that this book does not have permanent authority in the realm of morals. While the results of work on behalf of Moslems in the form of announced conversions have not been large, efforts of this kind have by no means been in vain, as is shown by the fact that a conference of Moslem converts was held recently in Zeitoun, Egypt. There are also among Moslems many secret believers in Christ, and it seems to be the general impression among missionaries that the time has come when we may expect to see an increasing number of conversions to Christianity among the Moslem population.

It is plain from what the missionaries write that by far the greatest progress of Christianity in Africa has been achieved within the past decade. Wherever there have been workers of holy life and strong faith to put in the sickle, they have gathered sheaves. This has been conspicuously exemplified in Uganda. There have been frequent revivals in that field during the past few years, but one of the most notable was that of March, 1906. During the eight days of special services the attendance increased steadily from 3500 on the first day to nearly 6000 on the last day. It was an ethical and spiritual movement. Bishop Tucker, in writing about it, says: " Drunkards signed the pledge in large numbers. Heathen enrolled themselves to such an extent as candidates for baptism that for a while it was difficult to arrange for their instruction, whilst the candidates for confirmation were so numerous that we were obliged to invade the Cathedral and hold our classes there, no fewer than thirteen such classes finding accommodation within its precincts. This large ingathering of souls through the special mission services at the capital was an indication of a similar ingathering which was going on more or less throughout the whole country." He estimates that during the five years ending September 30, 1907, fully 36,000 persons were baptized into the Church, or an average of more than 7000 each year. This wonderful Christward movement has continued in full tide, there being last year over 8000 new converts. An equally remarkable evangelistic movement has been going forward in Livingstonia, likewise in parts of the Congo Basin; but the mention of these fields must not exclude from view the fact that in other districts also the mighty working of the Spirit of God has been witnessed.

As one looks out over the non-Christian world, it is true that one may see some apparently barren fields and deserts, and observe certain sections and classes of the population in some countries which are not responding largely to the Gospel appeal; but taking the non-Christian world as a whole, the present is without doubt a time of rising spiritual tide. It is always wise to take advantage of a rising tide.

On the one hand, grave perils result if such a rising tide be not taken advantage of and wisely used. Many who have become interested, or impressed, or converted in the midst of the spiritual movement are in danger of lapsing and of passing into a state worse than that in which they were before they were awakened, unless by a continuation and enlargement of the spiritual efforts they are encouraged, guided, and built up. Moreover, unless the advantage is pressed, there is danger that many will stop just short of acting conclusively on the light which they have received or of responding to the spiritual impulses which they have felt; whereas, if advantage is taken of the favoring conditions, they may be led out into the path of obedience. Perhaps the greatest danger of all is that too many will press into the Christian Church before they have obtained sufficient training, and that the whole level of the Christian life of the community will thereby be lowered.

On the other hand, great victories are possible if only an adequate effort be made. Experience has shown that in improving such an opportunity far more can be accomplished within a short time than in a long period of persistent effort under other conditions. At such a time people are much more susceptible to religious impressions and more responsive to religious appeals. Moreover, a great opportunity is given to the Church of pressing out into its most difficult fields and of overcoming many of its most baffling obstacles. A great acquired momentum is essential for the accomplishment of such difficult ends, and what is a rising spiritual tide but an increasing momentum? What might not the Church have accomplished in the Telugu country during the past generation if it had pressed the advantage afforded by the first great revival which visited that field a generation ago? How different might have been the progress of Christianity among the high caste Hindus had the Church more largely utilized the advantage placed within its reach by the successful efforts put forth on their behalf by Alexander Duff? Some of the wisest students of missions believe that, as a result of the failure of the Church to improve its opportunity in Japan in the late eighties, the work of evangelizing that country has been greatly delayed and made more difficult. In every Christian land there have been solemnizing examples of the failure of the Church to take advantage of a rising spiritual tide. May Christians everywhere awaken to the fact that in the annals of Christianity there has been no time like the present. Surely it is a summons to the Church to put forth its strength in measure adequate to press the present unprecedented advantage.

THE REQUIREMENTS OF
THE PRESENT SITUATION:
AN ADEQUATE PLAN

CHAPTER IV

THE present changing and plastic condition of the non-
Christian nations, the forces at work which tend to
make the progress of Christianity increasingly difficult,
and the rising spiritual tide observable in many parts
of Asia and Africa combine to constitute an irresistible
call to the Christian Church to carry the Gospel to *all*
the non-Christian world before the present opportunity
passes away. Such an undertaking will make an
enormous demand upon the faith and resources of the
Church, for it is attended with difficulties which seem
almost insuperable. The number to be reached, embracing hundreds of millions, in itself shows that the
task is one of colossal proportions. Difficulties incident
to the climate, to the social condition of the people,
and to their stage of civilization are real and grave.
The fact that there are still over four hundred languages and dialects into which the Scriptures have not
been translated is a serious obstacle to the speedy
progress of the missionary enterprise. The strong
and persistent national prejudices and social antagonisms, the system of caste and other social restrictions
and divisions shut out the approach of the missionary;

and superstitions, corrupt practices, and active religious forces abound which strenuously oppose the teaching and spirit of Christianity. To evangelize the world, to change social and religious systems, and to reform the habits of thought and life of whole peoples, is a task that may well seem impossible. How is it to be accomplished? It is the first essential that the Church should have before it a plan adequate in scope, thoroughness, and strategy, to meet this unique world situation.

First, this plan should be adequate in scope. It should omit from consideration no region or people to which it is the duty of the Church to carry the Christian religion, and it must, therefore, at this time take the whole non-Christian world into its view. Time was when only a small part of the world was known and missionary work was limited in extent, but the field open to missionary work has widened immeasurably during the past century. There is scarcely one region in the world which is not open to-day to the Christian Gospel, and there is no nation to which it is not the immediate duty of the Christian Church to carry it. Christianity belongs to no particular nation or people; by virtue of the character, work, and command of its Founder, it is the only religion for all mankind. Nevertheless there are still, even so many centuries after Christ's coming to the earth, one thousand millions of non-Christian people, of whom probably not more than one-fifth have heard of Him with any degree of fulness and clearness. It is the Church's duty to see that this long-standing reproach is completely removed. Its plan of work, to be adequate, must provide for the evangelization of the whole of this multitude.

In the first place it must take account of the great unoccupied fields in the non-Christian world, for there are still vast regions without a single missionary. In the heart of Asia is a large integral area, almost equal in extent to the United States without its territories, and with an estimated population of 26,000,000, or more than half of that of the British Isles, which is almost without a messenger of Christianity. This great area includes Afghanistan, with its 4,000,000 of people, a population as large as that of Ireland; Bokhara, with over 1,000,000; Russian Turkestan, with at least 5,000,000 of Mohammedans; Tibet, with its 6,000,000 of people; Bhutan and Nepal, with a combined population of over 5,000,000; portions of Mongolia having a nomadic population of at least 2,000,000, and some of the other territories which are on the western fringe of China. In Southeastern Asia there is another extensive territory, comprising chiefly French Indo-China, with a population of over 20,000,-000, having in it but three or four Protestant missionary workers. Inland Africa, even more than Central Asia, is an unoccupied field. It contains various sections without missionaries, having in them an aggregate population of about 70,000,000, or more than that of Germany, Holland, Norway, and Sweden combined. This population of the unoccupied sections includes over 4,000,000 in the Sudan; fully 20,000,000 of the 30,000,000 of the Belgian Congo; 8,000,000 in the French Congo; 3,000,000 in the eastern part of Kamerun; 2,500,000 in Portuguese East Africa; 1,-700,000 in French Guinea; and 1,500,000 pagans in Eastern Liberia, besides a number of other large masses of people, each numbering over half a million, and being without any Christian worker.

There are several smaller unoccupied areas in different parts of the world; for example, the provinces of Nejd, Hejaz, and Hadramaut in Arabia, with a combined population of about 3,000,000. In these great and small areas there are 119,000,000 people who are without missionaries, and for the reaching of whom at present the Church has no plan.*

It is the belief of students of the present situation that a number of the totally unoccupied areas remote from present missionary operations might be entered by the Church in response to wise, concerted, and prayerful effort. That which is most needed is a large and comprehensive view on the part of present-day missionary leaders and an agreement among them on some plan which actually embraces the whole non-Christian world. If this can be obtained, other things needful will more readily follow; men who have a policy to carry out will insist upon finding some method by which to accomplish it. The older and more thoroughly established and resourceful societies will be urged to enlarge their activities, to include within their field some of the more remote unoccupied areas, and, if they are not able to respond so as to send men

* For a more adequate discussion of unoccupied fields, see "Unoccupied Mission Fields," by Samuel M. Zwemer.

to every nation, new societies may be established in order that this may be more promptly done.

Quite as significant as the integral unoccupied areas to which attention has been called are the multitudes of people unreached by the Gospel message who are living in territories adjoining fields in which missionaries are already working. Investigations instituted by Commission I of the World Missionary Conference afford ground for the impression that the population of these more accessible areas adjacent to present missionary forces exceeds that of the totally unoccupied sections. These men and women present in many ways the most extensive, the most pressing, and the most pathetic need of the missionary world—because the Gospel, which is the power of God unto salvation, is so near and yet so remote from them. Undoubtedly an increased missionary staff will be required before this need can be fully met, but it is the conviction of many that the large majority of the multitudes of unevangelized people living within the spheres of influence of missions already established might be reached with the Gospel, were these missions to expand their work with energy and thoroughness. In order that as effective use as possible may be made of the missions already established, the whole field should be surveyed and the responsibilities of each society to its own sphere of influence carefully and authoritatively determined. If this were done, overlapping would be avoided, new efforts would be made to rise to the responsibilities, and at least part of the at present unoccupied fields would quickly be evangelized.

Even in those parts of the non-Christian world where the number of missionaries, native Christian leaders, and Christian church members is largest, and where their influence is most potent and far-reaching, there is need of revising and enlarging the plans so as to embrace the entire population. It is maintained that in Japan, which has relatively a large staff of Christian workers in proportion to the population, less than one in ten of the people have heard the Gospel. In many fields the sowing has been in patches rather than broadcast. In some countries the cities have been largely evangelized, whereas the villages and rural districts have been almost wholly neglected. In other fields, where an extensive work of evangelization has been carried forward from the cities as bases, the cities themselves have been too much neglected. In both situations, while the neglect has been due in part to insufficient resources, in many cases it has been due also to lack of plan. Where all the Christian leaders have united in the aim to reach every person in their district within a given time, and to present the message with such intelligence, frequency, and thoroughness as to make it effective, the advantages of a plan have been at once evident. It is in these districts that the work of evangelization is being conducted most successfully and with the greatest completeness.

In almost every country certain strata or whole classes of society are being overlooked. An adequate plan must correct this by embracing them all. As an illustration of how classes of the population may be comparatively neglected in a country relatively well occupied by missionaries, attention is called to a statement, based upon a careful study by a company of eminent missionaries and Japanese leaders of some of those thus unreached in Japan. The following is the impressive list which they give: the rapidly increasing number of factory employees now numbering over three-quarters of a million; the still more numerous classes of artisans and day laborers; the nearly 100,000 railway employees; shopkeepers and merchants, numbering possibly one-sixth of the population; the men in the army and navy, aggregating 300,000 in active service; the aristocracy and men of wealth; and the poor and unlettered fishermen, scattered in villages and numbering in all perhaps 1,000,-000. In China, among the classes which have been almost entirely neglected are the men of wealth and the officials, and to an even greater extent their wives and children; the *literati* and modern government students, these last two classes notwithstanding the success which has always rewarded efforts made on their behalf; the aboriginal tribes, numbering about 6,000,000; the boat population, numbering millions; the Manchus; clerks and apprentices in shops; soldiers; the defectives; lepers. There is no adequate excuse for the neglect of so many entire classes. The comparatively limited resources of the missionary societies are no sufficient explanation of the fact that these classes have scarcely been touched. A special effort to influence any one of them would have had its effect, since experience in different parts of the world shows that when the Church concentrates itself on a given class, the effort is as a rule productive. It is believed, therefore, that the reason for the neglect is lack of recognition of the needs of these classes and of commensurate plans on their behalf.

The plan of the Church should take special account of the most difficult fields of the non-Christian world. While it is obviously wise to push forward the work along the lines of least resistance, it is not only bad policy, but it is disloyalty to the Lord Jesus Christ to neglect the regions which are most dangerous and most difficult. It is high time that the Church deliberately and resolutely attack some of these hitherto almost impregnable fortresses. This requires that the plan of the Church concern itself far more than heretofore with the reaching of the Mohammedan world. Moreover, there must be a wise policy of occupation of fields where the climate is peculiarly dangerous to foreigners. As the Rev. A. Taylor of the British and Foreign Bible Society has well said, " The risks to be faced and the personal dangers form no valid reasons for holding back. On the contrary, such sacrifices as have already been made have not been without their large effects, and, in addition, the record of them has been to many zealous souls an inspiring call. All possible advantage should be taken of the experience bought at so great a cost. Every valley must be exalted and every mountain and hill laid low, but there are also waste places— marsh or morass—through which the highway can only be made by the sacrifice of lives. The sacrifice must none the less be made. Policy or plan merely directs the course of sacrifice; it must be along the surveyed track. It ceases to be a waste of life and effort if at last the highway is firm under foot."

These neglected parts are so many and so large that the demands upon the Church will be far greater than it is immediately able adequately to meet. In spite of the great need, however, of a speedy advance, any tendency to hasten over the ground too quickly must be rigidly checked.

The plan of world evangelization should be adequate in point of thoroughness as well as in scope. There is no warrant in the teaching of Christ, nor in the practice of the early Christian Church for a superficial propagation of Christianity. Time will be gained and victory best ensured by doing the work in a most thorough manner. We are not simply to announce a message but to make genuine disciples of Christ. There could be no more serious danger for the Church itself than the spreading of an imperfect type of Christianity, due to ill-considered and careless plans, and to hasty and imperfect work in proclaiming, making plain, and enforcing the truth of Christ. A distinguished soldier, who had made a careful study of the war between Russia and Japan, said, " This war has borne into my mind in a way that nothing else could have done, the conviction that nothing but the very best will do." How much more true it is that in the conflict of Christianity with the non-Christian religions, the greatest thoroughness in the making and execution of plans is required. A review of the mission fields and methods with a view to the accomplishment of the world-wide missionary duty of the Church accentuates the importance of careful study of the problems involved in the world's evangelization. The consideration of the historic development of missions in their extension and method is the foundation of all wise advance. Such study of the present problems and of the historical development of missions is fundamental to the wisest and most thorough planning. The missionary movement to-day, possibly more than ever before, calls for thinkers and for missionary statesmen.

The campaign should also be adequate in strategy. There are strategic races, nations, and regions, the reaching of which for Christ and the Church will simplify the problem of reaching peoples elsewhere. The Chinese race is a good illustration. Its population of 400,000,000 constitutes one-fourth of the human race. It is located in the zone of power " where man has attained his highest development physically and mentally." It has preserved its integrity through its unbroken history of 4000 years, and with such national stability it combines the characteristics which have marked the greatest races—industry, frugality, patience, tenacity, great physical vigor, intellectual vigor as well, independence, and conservatism. The Chinese are moreover great colonizers, and have already gone out and established themselves on all the continents and in many of the Pacific Islands. They have been called the " Anglo-Saxons of the Orient," and destiny indeed seems to have fitted them to play as great a part in the future of the world as the Anglo-Saxons have played in the past. In bringing Christ to this

CONFERENCE OF THE CHINESE STUDENTS' CHRISTIAN ASSOCIATION, HARTFORD, CONN.

people, therefore, the Church is not only directly reaching one-third of the unevangelized population of the world, but is also indirectly influencing the future of Christianity in other parts of the world.

There are a number of principles that should govern the strategy of the Church in determining the order in which it should concentrate its attention upon different fields. No attempt is made to give them in order of their relative importance, because this must necessarily vary with each particular case. They are: (1) Accessibility, openness, and willingness to attend to the Gospel message. During the past ten years the peoples of pagan Africa have been peculiarly ready to listen to the presentation of the facts and arguments of the Christian religion. (2) The responsiveness of the field. Korea and Manchuria are examples of nations in which the people of every community show readiness to yield to the claims of Christ when presented to them. (3) The presence or concentration of large numbers of people. Obviously, the Chengtu plain of the westernmost province of China, with its population of 1700 to the square mile, or the densely populated valleys of the Ganges and lower Nile, should receive attention commensurate with the massing of the people. (4) Previous neglect. With a Gospel intended for all mankind the policy of the Church should be influenced by the existence of any totally unoccupied field, like extensive tracts of the Sudan. (5) Conditions of gross ignorance, social degradation, and spiritual need. Christ came in a special sense to seek and to save that which was lost, and the history of the Christian Church has abundantly shown how the blessing of God has attended efforts to reach the most unfortunate and depressed classes and peoples, such as the Pacific Islanders, the outcastes of India, the lepers, and the aboriginal tribes of the East Indies. (6) As has already been made plain, the Church, while recognizing the importance of advancing along lines of largest immediate promise, should, under divine guidance, direct special attention to the most difficult fields of the non-Christian world. In the light of this principle Moslem lands present an irresistible appeal to the Church. (7) The prospective power and usefulness of a nation as a factor in the establishment of Christ's Kingdom in the world, and the probable weight of its example as an influence over other nations. Japan is especially fitted to become in intellectual and moral matters, no less than in material civilization, the leader of the Orient. This attaches transcendent importance to its attitude toward Christianity. (8) The principle of urgency should as a rule have the right of way; that is, if there is to-day an opportunity to reach a people or section which in all probability will soon be gone, the Church should enter the door at once; for example, if there is a danger that the field may be pre-occupied by other religions or by influences adverse to Christianity. Equatorial Africa in a most striking degree is just now such a battle-ground. It is plain to every observer that unless Christianity extends its ministry to the tribes throughout this part of Africa the ground will in a short time be occupied by Mohammedanism.

Commission I of the World Missionary Conference

has sought to apply these principles to the missionary problems of the present day. The following extract from the findings which they submitted to the Conference as the result of their deliberations is, therefore, of great interest and significance:

" The Commission would direct attention to the following fields as of special urgency in respect of the prosecution of missionary work:

" 1. Fields on which *the Church as a whole* should concentrate attention and effort.

"(a) In China there is at this moment a unique opportunity which is fraught with far-reaching issues for the future not only of China and of the whole East, but also of Christendom.

"(b) The threatening advance of Islam in Equatorial Africa presents to the Church of Christ the decisive question whether the Dark Continent shall become Mohammedan or Christian.

"(c) The national and spiritual movements in India, awakening its ancient peoples to a vivid consciousness of their needs and possibilities, present a strong challenge to Christian missions to enlarge and deepen their work.

"(d) The problems of the Mohammedan World, especially in the Near East, which, until recently, received little consideration from the Church at large, have been lifted unexpectedly into prominence and urgency, as well as into new relations, by the marvelous changes which have taken place in Turkey and Persia. One of the important tasks before the Church at this time is to deal adequately with these problems.

" 2. Fields which do not claim the attention of the
Church as a whole, but which demand additional effort
on the part of the Societies already in some measure
occupying them:

" In Korea an evangelistic movement extending
rapidly over the land calls for a great strengthening of
the missionary force. In Japan the mission work
which has been centered in the great towns and among
the higher middle classes requires to be expanded effectively over the country, and among all classes. In
Malaya, Christian missions must strain every nerve to
prevent Islam from gaining the heathen tribes, and to
win them for Christ. Siam and Laos also present an
urgent appeal for an aggressive advance. In Mela-
nesia, a multitude of tribes in New Guinea, and other
islands, are opening in quick succession to Christian
influences. In various fields of pagan Africa, the
Christian missions which have been planted are confronted by immense opportunities among those who
are waiting for Gospel teaching, but who cannot be
reached by the forces now on the field.

" The rapid disintegration of the animistic and
fetishistic beliefs of primitive peoples in most of the
lands in the preceding lists presents an important problem. Most of these peoples will have lost their ancient
faiths within a generation, and will accept that culture-
religion with which they first come in contact. The
responsibility of the Church is grave to bring the Gospel to them quickly, as the only sufficient substitute
for their decaying faiths."

In view of the present comparatively limited resources of the missionary societies many Christian leaders unite in the belief, not only that the fields emphasized in the foregoing finding are of special urgency, but also that the relative order in which the Church should concentrate attention upon them is given in the order of sequence of the fields named in the two lists of this finding. *But the present resources of the Missionary Societies are not a measure of the latent resources of the Church.* Such boundless, though as yet unrealized resources should not be overlooked in determining the plan for the evangelization of the world. The following conviction, expressed by the Commission at the end of the second finding, is based upon this vital consideration:

" The enumeration of these fields might seem to suggest that the Church is not able to deal adequately and simultaneously with the entire non-Christian world. But the Commission declines to concede that this is so. After facing the facts, we share the conviction of the large majority of our correspondents that the Church of Christ, if it puts forth its strength, is well able to carry the Gospel to all these fields immediately. While we recognize the greater urgency in the case of certain fields, we find it impossible in the light of the needs of men, the command of Christ, and the resources of the Church, to delay giving to any people the opportunity to learn of Him. The point of chief emphasis is, that what the Church expects to do anywhere it must do soon. What is needed is a regular, sustained advance all along the line, in which all agencies shall be utilized and multiplied until they

are co-extensive with the need of the entire world."
This well expresses the urgent duty of the Church.

An adequate strategy recognizes that there are strategic classes as well as strategic races and nations. Prominent among these are the students of the non-Christian world, and of the Roman and Greek Catholic countries. There are at present over 500,000 students in the government institutions of higher learning in Asia alone, and were the number of students in mission schools and private institutions added, the total would be greatly augmented. In addition to these are large and increasing numbers of students in Africa and other parts of the non-Christian world. The German proverb should be borne in mind, "What you would put into the life of a nation, put into its schools." The schools, colleges, and universities are training the leaders of these nations. The teacher and the scholar wield a larger influence, if possible, in the East than in the West. The various learned professions are in their hands; they are laying the foundations and rearing the structure of Western civilization; in some of these lands they are the dominant factor in the political life, while in all non-Christian countries their political influence is steadily increasing. As already seen, the influence of Western learning has been in the direction of undermining the faith of the student class in the non-Christian religions and of breaking up the social and ethical restraints of the old civilizations. As a result, in many parts of the non-Christian world, the students, as a class, are drifting into agnosticism or indifference to religion. In such countries also as Russia

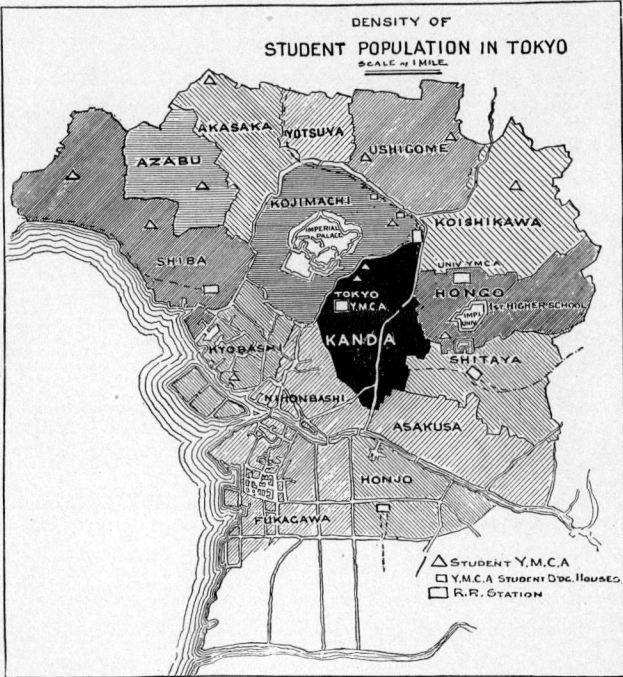

DENSITY OF
STUDENT POPULATION IN TOKYO
SCALE of 1 MILE

ΔStudent Y.M.C.A
☐ Y.M.C.A Student B'dg. Houses
☐ R.R. Station

There are fully 100,000 university, college and high-school students in Tokyo. It is estimated that there are over 20,000 in the Kanda Ward alone.

and the South American Republics the students, as a class, are virtually without religion. On the other hand, the introduction of Western learning has opened the minds of the students of Asia and Africa to the religious as well as to the other truth which the West has to bring. Nothing could be more important, therefore, from the point of view of successful strategy than reaching the student class for Christ. No part of missionary effort has been more fruitful in proportion to the attention and strength expended upon it than Christian work for the educated classes. This is especially true of those phases of work in which the Christian students have been organized to work among their fellow students.

The commercial classes should receive larger attention on the part of the missionary movement. One of the most pressing problems of missions is that of developing self-supporting churches, for it is essential to the wide and permanent extension of Christianity that the native Church should be free from dependence on foreign support. Until it is independent, it will not have the resources to do extensive work among the people of its own nation, nor will it feel its full responsibility to do such work. But if self-support is an essential, special effort must be made to win the commercial classes, since the obtaining of the necessary funds is largely dependent upon enlisting their interest, sympathy, and co-operation. It is too true that in most mission fields these classes have been hitherto largely unreached by missionary effort, but this is for the most part the fault of the Church and its

methods.   It is encouraging to note that wherever the
Church has adapted its methods to reach these classes,
they have been appreciative and responsive.

In considering the strategy involved in enlisting for
the plans of the Kingdom certain classes, the mistake
should not be made of confining attention exclusively
to those more favored and influential. This would be
to overlook the deep lesson of Christ's own practice
and the teaching of Church history, that if the cause
of Christianity is to be widely pervasive and triumphant in any country, it must lay strong hold on the lower
classes or masses.   Dr. J. P. Jones, of Madura, India,
aptly expresses this truth: " I believe that the masses
and not the classes should receive our greatest care.
It is no disgrace to Christianity, indeed it is its glory,
that it has, for the last 2000 years, first reached and
transformed the lower strata of society, and has passed
on through such to the highest, in its influence and
potency. It is doing the same thing in India to-day,
and its growing influence over the outcastes is one of
the healthful and sure signs of the ultimate dominance
of our faith in that land. By bringing them to Christ,
the whole fabric of Hindu society will be undermined
and will soon topple over, and there will be a great ingathering of the classes of India into the Kingdom of
our Lord."

From the early days of Christianity, the Church in
its strategy has recognized the wisdom of concentrating
its attention upon strategic places.   Any cause, to
possess a country, must concern itself with the centers
of political, commercial, educational, and social im-

portance and influence. Such strategy is pre-eminently called for in those countries of the non-Christian world, such as China and Japan, which have many large cities. It would be difficult to overstate the importance of establishing the Christian forces and institutions in great strength in a city like Tokyo, which in a very true sense dominates the Japanese Empire. A statesmanlike, constructive, and thoroughly spiritual work in Constantinople or Cairo will exert an influence throughout the vast Mohammedan world. An impressive object-lesson of what Christianity can do, if it is given in gateway cities like Shanghai, Bombay, and Rio de Janeiro, will affect entire countries. Years ago the Rev. J. Hudson Taylor, the founder of the China Inland Mission, worked out in a masterly way the plan of so locating the missionary forces as to influence most widely all China. The following is his own description of the plan which has, in the main, been carried out by that Mission: " All the operations of the Mission are systematic and methodical, and in accordance with the integral parts of one general and comprehensive plan for the evangelization of the whole of China; the aim of the Mission being, not to secure in a short time the largest number of converts for the China Inland Mission from a limited area, but to bring about in the shortest time the evangelization of the whole empire, regarding it of secondary importance by whom the sheaves may be garnered. Thus, in occupying a new province, the first station, if practicable, is opened in the capital, though it is well known that this is the most difficult place in the province in which to gather a church. The next step is, if possible, to open stations in the chief prefectures, then in subordinate ones, leaving, as a rule, places of less importance to be occupied later on. If the staff thus needed were concentrated in a country district, a large number of converts might be expected in a few years; but the influence of these country Christians would not be likely to extend beyond the boundary of their own villages. By the before-mentioned plan, centers are opened from which the Gospel may be diffused throughout the whole extent of a province."

In all consideration of missionary strategy, one of the questions demanding solution is that of the proper distribution of the missionary forces. Strategy concerns itself not only with the country to be entered and the forces which oppose, but also with the forces to be wielded in the campaign and with the resources at their disposal. The experience throughout the mission field suggests certain guiding principles as to how best to utilize the comparatively insufficient yet valuable forces at the disposal of the Church, so as to make Christ known to the largest possible number of people and to build up strong and enduring churches.

(1) One factor in determining the distribution of the missionary forces is the density of the population to be evangelized. Wherever the population is very sparse, as among the nomads of Central Asia or in parts of Africa, there is no need of concentrating a large number of workers at the mission stations; it is more desirable that they should be distributed over a wide area. Quite different is the situation in densely

populated countries like Japan and the larger part of China, where large cities, whose influence radiates over the surrounding districts and neighboring villages, provide great opportunities for mission work. In such regions the plan should be to establish strong stations, adequately manned. Even in such densely populated districts, however, missionary leaders have advocated two different lines of policy. Some have advised that the mission concentrate its attention on the building up of the Christian community which is already under its influence, and on the training of native Christian workers in order to have them do the work of evangelization in the outlying regions. This may be described as the policy of concentration. Other leaders have advocated that the mission should direct its efforts mainly to the surrounding non-Christian peoples with the view of evangelizing the whole region as speedily as possible. This may be called the policy of diffusion. These two policies are, however, not permanently in conflict. One of them must invariably lead into the other before any district can be completely evangelized. The policy of concentration, when effectively followed, must result in wide evangelization by the native workers who have been trained up for this purpose. On the other hand, the policy of diffusion, if successful in influencing a large number to become Christians, makes it important to follow up the work by instructing the inquirers, organizing the converts into churches, and training them for Christian service. Which of the two policies is to be followed first is one of the problems which ought to be solved in any adequate plan.

(2) The temperamental characteristics, the state of culture, and the religion of the people to be evangelized, have much to do with determining the proper distribution of the forces. It makes a great deal of difference whether the people are ignorant and superstitious tribes in the heart of Africa, or whether they constitute the highly civilized inhabitants of the more enlightened parts of the Orient, who may, in addition, have availed themselves of Western education. The former will not require a missionary staff so large, nor one including so many experts as will the latter. The great and highly organized religions present a stronger resistance than the simpler nature-worship of barbarous tribes, and they would therefore require a larger and better-equipped staff of workers. Perhaps it might be laid down as an axiom that whatever force is stationed in a district ought to be of sufficient strength and adequacy of equipment to make itself strongly felt in spite of all the difficulties.

(3) Another factor which largely influences the disposition of the forces is the number and character of the native Christian workers and the strength of the native Church. As the native leaders become able to administer the native Church and care for it spiritually, the missionaries are relieved of a great responsibility and can thus devote themselves more largely to extending the missionary movement into unevangelized regions. At the same time the most highly multiplying work which the missionary can do, in the interest of accomplishing the evangelization of a country, is that of raising up and training an adequate staff of native

workers and of communicating to them the evangelistic
spirit.

(4) Another principle which some missions are
prone to overlook is that of readjusting the mission
forces from time to time in order better to meet changing conditions. The present situation in China and
Japan, for example, is entirely different from that
which existed at the time when the missionaries were
obliged to reside in a few city centers, and concentrate
the entire missionary forces in these. When later the
revision of the treaties made it possible for missionaries to reside and work in the interior, some of the
missions adjusted themselves to the changed conditions,
but since then conditions have very largely changed
again. There is need that the foreign and native leaders on each mission field should make a fresh study of
the present distribution of the forces with a view to
bringing about any further needed adjustments and
enlargements.

Quite as important as the plan, no matter how well
devised and no matter how great the forces for carrying it into execution, is the spirit in which it is con-
ceived and with which it is carried out. It calls for a
spirit of unwearying patience, of great intensity, of contagious enthusiasm, of undaunted heroism, of triumphant faith, and of Christlike sympathy. Moreover, the
hope of real success in taking the Gospel to all the non-
Christian world in our day is in a campaign characterized by the spirit of unity. God is unmistakably sum-
moning the missionary forces of the Church, both at
home and abroad, to a larger and truer unity. It would

seem that at such a time of opportunity and crisis as
the present, the overlapping, friction, and waste resulting from the lack of unity is nothing less than griev-
ously sinful.   Much can and ought to be done to avoid
such overlapping, which is evidenced not only in establishing mission stations in the same neighborhood, but
also in duplicating different branches of work, such as
colleges, hospitals, and mission printing-presses.   It
may be that this will involve apparent sacrifice, some
uprooting and transplanting, and much mutual consideration on the part of different missionary societies
working in the same field, but this should not be
allowed to interfere with greater efficiency.   It is believed by students of the missionary problem that a
comprehensive plan of co-operation in the missionary
work of the various Christian communions, entered
into and carried out in a realizing sense of our oneness
in Christ, would be the equivalent of doubling the missionary forces.   The Commission on Co-operation and
the Promotion of Unity, in their Report at the World
Missionary Conference, voiced in the following
language the convictions of a large and rapidly increasing number of Christians throughout the world,
both as to the urgent necessity of such a unity and as
to the real secret of realizing it:

" The time is short; the day of our opportunity is
limited.   These intellectual, moral, and social revolutions are taking place with unprecedented rapidity.
And it is more than ever incumbent on the Christian
Church to realize its responsibility to carry the Gospel
to the lands which are now open to receive it, and to

guide the awakening nations to God in Christ. For the accomplishment of this overwhelming task it seems essential that the Christian Church should present a united front. Its divisions are a source of weakness and impair the effectiveness of its testimony to the one Gospel of the Son of God which it professes. The issues are so great that there can be no trifling in the matter. The evangelization of nations, the Christianizing of empires and kingdoms, is the object before us. The work has to be done now. It is urgent and must be pressed forward at once. The enterprise calls for the highest quality of statesmanship, and for the maximum of efficiency in all departments of the work. It is not surprising that those who are in the front of this great conflict, and on whose minds and souls the gravity of the issues presses most immediately, should be the first to recognize the need for concerted action and closer fellowship. . . . The Churches in the mission field may lead the way to unity; but they cannot move far and move safely without the co-operation of the Church at home. The great issues which confront us in the modern situation are the concern of the whole Church of Christ; and the spiritual resources of the whole Church will be required to deal with them. The solution of problems so complex and difficult and so vitally related to the advancement of the Kingdom of Christ, can be attempted only in a spirit of penitence and of prayer. Penitence is due for the arrogance of the past and for the lack of sympathy and of insight by which all of us have helped to create and perpetuate a situation that retards so seriously the advancement of

Christ's Kingdom.   Most of all do we need to lament
that we carry about with us so small a sense of the
harm that is wrought by our divisions, and so little
pain for our lack of charity.   Prayer is needed, because
human wisdom can discern no remedy for the situation. . . . Whether we have regard to the union
and federation of native churches, or to the reaching
of agreements between different Missions, or to the
working of schemes of co-operative effort, we believe
that the real problem to be faced is a moral one.
Schemes of co-operation sometimes break down, because the basis on which they are attempted is an impossible one; but more often the failure lies in ourselves.   If the movement toward unity in the mission
field is to gather strength and volume, the supreme need
is not for schemes of union, but, as has been well said,
for apostles of unity.   Men are needed with sufficient
largeness of mind and breadth of sympathy to understand the point of view of those with whom they co-
operate.   Most of all, men are needed who have seen,
and who can lead others to see, the vision of unity;
men who know that love is the fulfilling of the law, and
who have a living faith that God is able to do exceed-
ing abundantly above all that we ask or think."

THE REQUIREMENTS OF THE
PRESENT SITUATION:
AN ADEQUATE HOME BASE

CHAPTER V

COMMISSION I of the World Missionary Conference, in
the course of its inquiry into the problem of carrying
the Gospel to all the non-Christian world, conducted
correspondence with several hundreds of leading missionaries in all parts of the world, as well as with
leaders of the Church in Christian lands, and, among
other questions, asked what constitutes the most crucial
problem in connection with the great missionary task.
It is a remarkable fact and one that gives cause for
much reflection, that to this question the larger proportion of the correspondents, although face to face with
all the difficulties of the work abroad, agree in reply-
ing, " The state of the home Church." They feel
that the apathy and indifference manifested to-day
among Christians at home are the greatest discouragements and hindrances to the extension of the missionaries' work. Any plan such as has been outlined in
the last chapter will be comparatively useless if there
be not a great advance in the home field in missionary
interest, spirit, and activity, for it is on the home
Church that the foreign work depends for its inspiration, guidance, and support. It is of the first im-

portance, therefore, that we consider the factors essential to the home Church, if it is to form an adequate directing and supporting base of the missionary effort abroad.

The first is an able leadership of the missionary forces on the home field. No movement more than that of foreign missions demands the ablest leaders. The magnitude of this enterprise calls for men of large capacity to lead it. The peculiar complexity and difficulty of the problems to be solved, concerning as they do so many races, religions, and social conditions, can be met only by men of vision and of great directive power. The fact that the missionary movement must be projected and conducted at long range makes it essential that its leadership be intrusted only to men of the highest qualifications. As modern missions are a comparatively recent undertaking and as there are still so many fields virtually unentered, able men are needed to set the right precedents and to lay secure foundations. For the sake of the missionaries at the front, men who can and will command their confidence and devoted following are indispensable. Too little attention has in the past been paid to secure the right men for this work, and the missionary movement has suffered accordingly. The fact that a more triumphant advance is not being made in parts of the non-Christian world in the face of most inspiring opportunities is due largely to a lack of wise and sufficient directive energy at the home base.

The leaders demanded must be men of clear and strong convictions as to the absolute need and infinite importance of the missionary enterprise and the peculiar urgency of the present situation. They must be men of originality and courageous initiative, able to guide both in pioneer and constructive processes. They must have the power and disposition to think through the plans and problems and to master baffling conditions. To a rare degree they need the gift of imagination in order to see the foreign conditions and to place themselves at the point of view of those whom they are to serve. They should have power to inspire the confidence and to arouse the enthusiasm of the lay and clerical leaders in the home Church, and, especially at this stage of the missionary enterprise, should be men of breadth, insight, and sympathy, qualified to develop along wise lines the growing movements of co-ordination, co-operation, federation, and union. In a word, the leadership of modern missions requires seers, thinkers, statesmen.

In addition to able leaders to guide the operations of the missionary societies of the different Christian communions, there is need of an able leadership in the various churches, parishes, or congregations. In a later section the important part to be taken by laymen will be specially emphasized. Without doubt, however, it is true that the Christian ministry holds the key to the missionary problem. If the clergy are keenly interested in foreign missions, if they are aflame with the missionary passion, if they believe that there is no other work more important than that of leading the forces of the Church to the conquest of the world for Christ, then the larger part of the problems of missions, which depend so much for their solution on the intelligent and devoted backing of the communicant church membership, will be solved. Much more attention must be paid to giving the subject of foreign missions its proper place in all the home theological seminaries. And even in addition to this there should be more comprehensive and constant efforts to cultivate the missionary interest in the schools, and also in the young people's societies of the Church, from which the ranks of the Christian ministry are recruited.

Leadership, however, is not confined to the missionary boards and the clergy. Those who lead in the work of the young people of the Church may play an equally important part in the missionary movement, for it is from them that the future leaders of the Church, clerical and lay, are being raised up, and men and women enlisted to carry on its varied activities. In the end it is by young people that young people are led, and in every congregation there is need for men and women who will lead their fellows into an active interest in missions. Any one who has the power of leadership, and will take upon himself this responsibility, may play an important part in the world's evangelization.

The work of the Young People's Missionary Movement and of various other organizations and movements among young men and young women of the different Christian communions is, therefore, of fundamental importance, involving as it does the raising up of the clerical and lay leadership of the Church and the enlisting of others who are to carry on its varied

A YOUNG PEOPLE'S MISSIONARY MOVEMENT CONFERENCE AT SILVER BAY, N. Y.

activities. The workers and members in all these
societies should bear in mind that in doing well the
work in which they are engaged in the realms of mission study, of Bible study, of social service, of promoting the cause of missions by enlisting interest, gifts,
and intercession, they are not only directly accomplishing great good, but also are indirectly rendering a
valuable service to the Church in affording a school of
practical training for meeting the responsibilities which
await them in the missionary work of the Church.
Conferences of workers among young people, especially
secretaries, for developing missionary interest among
young people, and any other methods of improving the
leadership of the young people's work in the different
parishes, are all helping in a most practical way to
realize the missionary purpose of the Church.

In addition to the need for leaders a far larger number of missionary candidates than is now forthcoming
is required to meet the present situation. Some missionary societies are experiencing difficulty in finding
even a sufficient number to fill the gaps in the missionary ranks caused by death or by furloughs enforced
by breakdown in health, and yet everywhere there is
an urgent demand for an actual increase in the staff.
More workers from the home lands are needed to
press into the great unoccupied regions adjoining fields
where work is already being carried on, and there are
still totally unoccupied countries calling for heroic
pioneers. The very success of the work in all parts
of the world has, moreover, made imperative a great
extension of present missionary operations, in order

that the Church may reap the results which recent triumphs have made possible. There are but few mission fields already occupied which are not to-day clamoring for reinforcements, because the present staff cannot overtake the work that is already laid to its hand. Further, the unprecedented crises which we have seen to be simultaneously confronting the Church in so many parts of the field—crises on which the future of Christianity hinges so largely—present a unique appeal for more missionaries.

Of far greater importance, however, than the increase in the number of missionaries is it that men and women of high qualifications be secured and sent out to the non-Christian world. The foreign missionary service has always required, and more largely than most callings, has had, workers of high qualifications, but owing to the rapid spread of Western education in non-Christian lands, owing to the great social, intellectual, and religious changes and movements now in progress in those lands, owing to the greater complexity of missionary work, and owing to the critical situation now confronting Christianity, there is greater need than ever of exercising special care in the choosing and preparation of missionary candidates. Men of all-round qualifications and training are required. They should be men who have sound physical health, who are well-trained intellectually, and have the determination to preserve their habits of study. They should be open-minded and teachable. They should be able to work with others without friction. They should have in large measure the power of sympathy. As

many of them are to be teachers, trainers, superintendents, they should possess the gift of leadership.
They should be thoroughly established in their
belief in the fundamental points of the Christian faith,
and it is of the first importance that they have the missionary passion, the desire and purpose to devote themselves unselfishly to the service of others. Above all,
they should be men of spirituality, who have established securely those habits on which the maintenance
of an expanding spiritual life depends. In view of the
responsible work into which they are to go, we cannot set the ideal too high, and if it be impossible to find
many candidates who possess all of these traits and
talents, the effort must be made to approximate as
nearly as possible to the ideal.

It is of special advantage to the missionary in his
practical work to have had a university or college education, and it is plain, therefore, that the missionary
societies should regard the universities and colleges as
a principal recruiting ground for missionaries. In the
United States, Canada, Australasia, and South Africa
nearly all of the men missionary candidates and an increasing number of the women candidates are drawn
from the student classes, and in Great Britain this is
becoming more and more the case. The numbers of
university men in the mission field might be still further increased if greater efforts were made to enlist the
services of the younger ministers, physicians, teachers,
and others who have passed from the universities into
various spheres of work at home. Numbers of these
have entered upon work in which they have manifested

special adaptation for a missionary career and have acquired valuable experience for it. These might readily be persuaded to go out to work in a wider sphere.

Nevertheless, while there are marked advantages, other things being equal, in drawing missionary candidates from those who have had special educational preparation, it is important that those who belong to other classes should on no account feel themselves deterred from offering for service. On the continent of Europe a majority of the candidates do not come from the universities, but receive special training in institutions provided for the purpose, and it is the experience of many missionary societies that there are many young men and women who, while lacking the discipline of the higher education, yet possess in a rare degree many of the fundamental qualifications for missionary service, and who, with special training under the direction of the societies, may be prepared for an efficient missionary career. Not a few of those who have rendered conspicuous service never had great educational advantages ; for example, Robert Moffat was a gardener, and Robert Morrison, a maker of shoe-lasts. Moreover, now that the missionary enterprise has become so complex and therefore calls for workers possessing such a variety of special qualifications, there are opportunities to utilize men having practical experience for such positions as managers of printing offices, superintendents of the erection of buildings, mission treasurers, and business managers of educational institutions. But the essential qualification in all these is that they be men of deep spirituality in order that their personal influence may help in the work of evangelization. Young men and young women who are ambitious to place their lives where they will be most useful in the extension of Christ's Kingdom should be encouraged to qualify themselves for the missionary career. Every one who determines to do so can make himself or herself fit to be of service in the mission field, and every one who is willing to go and can pass the required examination is needed to-day.

Statistics show that in North America and Great Britain, as well as in Australasia and South Africa, the principal agency through whose instrumentality candidates have been obtained for the foreign field has been the Student Volunteer Movement. As a direct result of the work of this Movement in these countries there have gone out to the foreign field under the various missionary societies, within a little over twenty years, over 6,000 volunteers, of whom about two-thirds have gone from North America. By the use of traveling secretaries, by the promotion of mission study in the universities and colleges, through the circulation of effective missionary literature, through student conferences and missionary institutes, and by the promotion of intercessory prayer, this Movement has become increasingly efficient and fruitful. It is not in any sense a new missionary society, but directs its energies solely towards developing missionary interest among students and towards obtaining candidates for the mission field. In this way its chief function is to be an auxiliary agency to the missionary societies and to supply them with the candidates which they need. The usefulness of the Movement in North America has recently been greatly increased by the important step which it has taken of establishing a Candidates' Department, which serves as a clearing-house between the missionary societies and the candidates. It has secretaries in charge who acquaint themselves with the specific needs of the different missionary societies and bring to the attention of the boards students or others who might be able to meet these needs. The British Movement is establishing a similar department. This is in every way a wise step, and will make it much easier for the societies to find the right men for the right posts.

The Student Movement renders the further important service of trying to place upon every student who is to go out to the non-Christian world to engage in other than the missionary calling, a burden of responsibility for advancing the interests of Christ's Kingdom. Opportunities for such service are multiplying on every hand. A great many of the best engineering students and those connected with other departments of applied science are going in increasing numbers to lands like China, Africa, and Turkey to help in their industrial development. There is also a growing demand for students from America and Europe, both men and women, to go out to different parts of the non-Christian world to teach in government schools and colleges, and in other non-missionary institutions. Others also are sent out to fill positions in the diplomatic and consular service and in the various departments of the civil service.   It is almost impossible to overestimate the importance of these being men of genuine Christian character, and men who, by word and work, will not only safeguard the missionary interests committed to their charge, but will also throw the full weight of their influence on the side of Jesus Christ.   When one thinks of the great service rendered by such Christian civilians as Sir Andrew Fraser in India, Sir Mortimer Durand in Persia, President Taft in the Philippines, and Judge Wilfley in China, one recognizes the possibilities before young men who devote their lives with Christian purpose to the service of the Government in other lands, and one recognizes, too, how much is lost when the lives are not so devoted. In filling these men with the determination to make their influence tell for Christ, the Student Movement is doing a work scarcely less valuable than the raising up of an equal number of missionaries.

The Student Volunteer Movement occupies a position of unique importance, but its activity ought to be supplemented in as many other ways as possible. Secretaries of missionary societies, and also missionaries on furlough who are specially qualified to influence students by their visits to the different student communities and conferences, have frequent opportunities for exerting their influence.   The Young People's Missionary Movement, through the promotion of missionary intelligence among young people in the churches, including those in the Sunday schools, can, in close co-operation with the Volunteer Movement and the missionary societies, do much to enlist well-qualified men and women who are not students to devote themselves to the missionary career. Clergy, college professors, and schoolmasters are also in a position to do perhaps more than any other factor or agency to increase the supply of missionaries, because they are in constant touch with the sources of supply and can exert a unique influence upon the lives under their guidance. Christian ministers, in particular, in influencing the home life and the spiritual attitude of parents, can deal most effectively with one of the most difficult aspects of the problem of missionary supply. It has too often been the case that the indifference or the opposition of parents has been the means of hindering those who would otherwise have offered themselves for service in the foreign field.

Sunday school teachers, leaders of mission study classes, and others who greatly desire to see the number of suitable missionary candidates increased, can do much to get young people to consider thoroughly and conscientiously the claims of missionary service. One instance is reported where from one mission study circle alone no fewer than four members were led to volunteer to become missionaries, and the story of James Chalmers of New Guinea, whose first resolution to become a missionary was the result of an appeal made by his Sunday school teacher, is by no means an isolated case in the history of missions. The missionaries of the future are to be found among the Sunday school pupils of the present, and it is the duty, as well as the privilege, of the teachers to see that their number is greatly increased.

If all Christians who are given these places of opportunity were to use them wisely, a much larger number of candidates would be forthcoming; but if a supply, sufficient for the present need, is to be secured, the whole Christian Church must learn to employ with greater faithfulness the Christ-appointed means of securing laborers for the world-wide ripening harvest fields—the mighty force of intercession.

The same reasons which make necessary an increase in the number of missionary candidates obviously necessitate an increase in financial support. There is need of a large increase in gifts, because the multiplication of the number of missionaries involves, besides additional salaries, additional equipment and other enlargements of the work. The pressing opportunities which must be improved lest they be lost demand an early as well as a great increase in the financial resources. There is not a missionary society in the world which does not stand in need of more funds. Because of the lack of money some societies have actually been compelled in some places to abandon work which was full of promise.

Happily the members of the Christian Church are well able to supply all the funds needed. It is a striking fact that the wealthiest nations are the principal Christian nations. It is even more significant that a disproportionate share of the money in these countries has been intrusted to Christians. One of the most encouraging signs of these days is the growing recognition on the part of Christian men and women that they are trustees and in no sense sole proprietors, that they can-

not take their money out of the world with them, that
they are responsible not simply for a good use but for
the very best use of their money, that it is wise for
them to be their own executors, and that one of the
most productive uses of money is that of relating it to
the plans of the expanding Kingdom. The year 1909
witnessed the largest gift ever made to work on the
mission field namely, the bequest of over $4,000,-
000 in the will of Mr. John S. Kennedy, of New
York, to various foreign missionary objects. During the present year another Christian in the
same city has given $1,000,000 to foreign missions,
and there have been other large gifts to this object, possibly a greater number than in any one
year in the history of missions. Moreover, in some
Christian lands, it is still more encouraging to note the
growing volume of missionary contributions from
Christians possessing very small means. Although it
is hopeful to see that some who have great wealth are
being led to dedicate it to the propagation of the Gospel it is not chiefly to the wealthy that the Church must
look for the needed funds. The greater part of the
income of the missionary societies comes from the
large volume of contributions from those of smaller
means, and the need of the future is not so much large
occasional gifts as it is that the ordinary church member should be trained to give conscientiously, intelli-
gently, and systematically, with a full realization of
the needs which his gifts will help to meet.

Various methods have been used with this end in
view. A method of universal and permanent value,

absolutely essential to ensure gifts adequate in amount and prompted by the right spirit, is effective instruction from the pulpit on the subject of Christian stewardship and on scriptural habits of giving, especially the habit of systematic and proportionate giving, and giving as unto the Lord and not as unto men. Such instruction should be supplemented by the use of the most effective printed matter on the subject, and, above all, by actually inducing members of the church to adopt such principles. This latter, perhaps, can best be done by means of another most fruitful method, that of a personal canvass of the entire church membership, to enlist, if possible, some gift from each member. At the present time in most countries, with the exception of Germany, where the larger part of the income is derived from the church membership in village or rural parishes, it is safe to say that fully nine-tenths of the missionary funds are contributed by one-tenth of the church members, and that the remaining one-tenth of the funds comes from very considerably less than half of the remainder of the church members. That such a large proportion of Christian people have little or no concern about the missionary work of the Church is highly unsatisfactory and is doubtless due more to ignorance of the need of their help than to lack of Christian sympathy. Such a personal canvass, therefore, if conducted by those who appreciate and understand the missionary situation, might be the means of obtaining the support of many who, when they learn that it is their duty, will gladly give. Experience has shown that this canvass of the member-

ship will result in a much larger sum being secured
each year if it be conducted by committees rather than
by individuals.

Another plan which explains the increase in gifts in
many places has been that of getting individual parishes, young people's societies, families, and individual
church members, each to support one or more missionaries or some other special object. This plan has its
disadvantages, but the advantages associated with it,
especially the increased gifts which it calls forth, far
outweigh the disadvantages. Another method possibly
more desirable, and with fewer administrative difficulties, is known as the station plan. This plan involves
the relating of a given small constituency—a local
church or group of churches—to a specified station
abroad, through the agency of the mission board. The
advantage here is that while missionaries and native
staff change, the community which is being evangelized
remains, and the interest aroused in the sustaining
churches at home is thus likely to be more constant.

A successful method developed by several communions is known as the apportionment plan. According to
this plan a given communion, after deciding how much
money it will aim to secure for missions in a given year,
apportions the total sum among the various local parishes or congregations, so that each one will know its
assigned share of the total amount to be secured within
the year. In this way many local churches have been
led greatly to increase their contributions.

One of the most hopeful developments in the direction of increasing the support of foreign missions, as

well as in other directions, has been the inauguration of the Laymen's Missionary Movement. This Movement was organized in New York in 1906, and while it has since spread to Britain and one or two other countries, it has reached its highest efficiency in the United States and Canada. It is not a new missionary society to collect or administer funds or to send out missionaries. " It is an inspiration, not an administration." Its aim is to interest laymen in the subject of missions and to lead them to recognize and to accept their responsibility to promote the cause of missions in connection with the Christian communion to which they belong.

While it is interdenominational, its work is carried on through the channels of each Christian communion. To this end interdenominational co-operating committees of laymen are organized in the different communities. These committees ascertain the actual facts as to what is being done for missions by the different communions and by the city or town as a whole. They then arrange an opportunity for the presentation of these facts and of the claims of foreign missions to the laymen of all the churches of the community. It has usually been found advisable to have this done in connection with a great laymen's dinner. Before this gathering is arranged, separate denominational conferences are usually held, and on the basis of conclusions arrived at in them a definite policy as to the missionary activities of the community is drawn up. At the dinner this policy is presented, discussed, and adopted, and afterwards an interdenominational gathering of laymen is held for the discussion of practical methods for carrying out the programme agreed upon by the different churches. To help in carrying out the policy agreed upon, an energetic and efficient missionary committee is organized in each congregation. Interdenominational conventions or conferences were held in all the principal cities of Canada commencing with the year 1908, and during the winter of 1909-10 there were similar conventions in seventy-five of the leading cities of the United States as well as on a smaller scale in many other communities. In the accomplishment of its work the international Laymen's Missionary Movement employs a corps of able secretaries to direct the propaganda. Much use is made of missionary literature especially adapted to laymen. The movement began in a meeting for prayer, and, ever since, its chief reliance has been upon prayer. No subject receives such large attention in its conferences. The Movement has stimulated the plan of deputations of Christian laymen representing different denominations going out to visit the various mission fields, with reference to awakening on their return a wider interest among their fellow laymen. As a result of these methods the Movement has done more than any other one means to stir up interest among laymen and to enlarge their financial co-operation.

One of the best single illustrations of the financial results of the Movement is in connection with the Southern Presbyterian Church, the first to organize its own separate Laymen's Movement. It is, however, related to the interdenominational Movement as well.

DINNER OF THE LAYMEN'S MISSIONARY MOVEMENT IN NEW YORK

Four years ago the total contributions to foreign missions of that Church were $223,000. During that year their Laymen's Movement was organized. The next year the contributions increased to $275,000, the year following to $323,000, while last year they reached $412,000. Forty-eight of the individual churches of that denomination contributed on the average $4 per member to foreign missions.

The best illustration of the increased giving to missions in a large city under the direct influence of the Laymen's Movement is Toronto. The following table indicates the advances in annual receipts made in the five principal Christian communions in a period of two years:

	YEAR 1907	YEAR 1909
Anglican	$51,786.00	$71,000.00
Baptist	23,006.85	60,877.09
Congregational	3,339.00	4,963.00
Methodist	61,753.45*	102,754.24*
Presbyterian	46,332.13	111,611.00
	$186,217.43	$351,205.33

It is a striking fact that, contrary to the fears of some Church leaders, the gifts to the work of the Church in the home communities have increased along with those to foreign missions.

A more important result of the Laymen's Movement than the increase in financial support has been its influence in enlisting the laymen as advocates of and workers for foreign missions. Literally thousands of

* For the year closing April 30.

laymen throughout the United States and Canada who had no interest in the subject are now making speeches on missions, conducting mission study classes, guiding missionary organizations, and conducting financial canvasses. The Movement is thus helping to develop the lay leadership of the Church. Some consider that the most significant result of this Movement has been in the direction of promoting Christian unity, as a result of drawing together in spirit, planning, and aggressive effort the most active and influential laymen of the different communions.

Whatever methods of raising money are followed, the aim should be not so much the securing of gifts as the developing of the right motives and spirit in the givers. The greatly increased giving which is demanded by the present situation in the mission field cannot be obtained simply by urging people to give. The gifts will be adequate only when they flow spontaneously from men who have been moved by a consciousness of the world's need.

If we are to have able missionary leadership at home, intelligent adoption of the missionary calling as a lifework, financial support in proportion to the need, prayer with the spirit and with the understanding also, if we are to have the broadest and most virile types of Christian character in the membership of the Church, there must be a thorough promotion of missionary intelligence. This work has three main aims: The maintenance of interest among those who are already well-disposed, in order that there may be no falling off in the present giving, prayers, and missionary activi-

ties of the Church; the securing of additional supporters both among adults who are at present indifferent and especially among the rising generation;
the securing of a special body of missionary teachers,
campaigners, and other workers at home, and of suitable candidates for the foreign field. There has been
a wide-spread failure to recognize the importance of
the last two aims, and to employ methods adequate to
realize them.

For the general maintenance and growth of missionary interest the most widely used agencies are the
missionary sermon or address, the missionary meeting,
and the missionary magazine. These have rendered
great service, but in this age of increasing culture and
criticism and literary competition they all must be of
better quality than ever if they are to continue their
past achievements. Missionary books, news bulletins,
and the secular press should all be used freely to assist
in realizing this aim. The individuals who must take
the lead in this work are the pastors, the officials of
missionary societies, and missionaries on furlough.

When we consider methods for reaching those who
are not yet interested, it must be admitted that the
methods now in use are much less adequate. The average non-missionary church member will go out of his
way to avoid a missionary sermon or meeting or magazine. The number of new converts made by any of
these agencies each year is comparatively small. Plainly
they must be adapted and strongly supplemented before the present body of missionary supporters will
be largely increased. Three special needs may be men-

tioned; the need of securing an attentive hearing, the need of adaptation to special temperaments and types of thought, and the need of cumulative influences to overcome dense ignorance and prejudice. If these three needs can be met, we may hope not only to annex for the missionary enterprise great untouched fields of wealth and influence, but to fill vacant lives with an ideal worthy of their best endeavor.

To secure a hearing, we must depart from our traditional methods which in the minds of the indifferent are associated too often with dullness. We must provide more attractive meetings and advertise them with greater enthusiasm. The use of debates and dramatic programmes, lantern slides, and charts will help, provided their quality be good. The testimony of travelers will arouse the skeptical. A yet larger use should be made of the press and of secular magazines. Missionary exhibitions have proved most efficient in England, and are being transplanted to America. The Laymen's Missionary Movement has secured a hearing from many persons heretofore indifferent because it is big, businesslike, interdenominational, and enthusiastic. To many outsiders the foreign missionary enterprise seems like a small affair on account of our narrow and languid way of promoting it. Any evidence that we thought it worth strenuous action would at once compel their attention.

In reaching special temperaments, we must aim at one thing at a time. It would be well if we could sometimes grade our audiences. We need broad and thoughtful treatment for persons of special culture;

facts, figures, and problems for business men; fair-minded apologetic for the prejudiced and narrow. Brotherhood meetings for men and current events clubs for women should discuss such documents as the reports of the Edinburgh Conference, selecting the subjects of greatest interest. A multitude of individuals who have imagined the subject of foreign missions as necessarily dull would be amazed to discover the attractiveness to them of some of its phases.

To secure cumulative influences, nothing is better than the mission study class. It is surprising how often indifferent persons can be secured for membership by special effort. Attendance at summer conferences has transformed many skeptics into enthusiasts. We do not expect to arouse the careless with evangelistic influences without a carefully prepared and continued campaign. The reason why so many professing Christians are still indifferent to the subject of foreign missions is because the Church has never taken the trouble to reach them.

It would be difficult to overstate the importance of the missionary education of children and young people. Fortunately we now have at our disposal the results of years of child study by specialists, which must obviously be mastered as a preliminary. Missions must take its place as an essential part of the Sunday school curriculum to be taught as a modern Acts of the Apostles. This agency may need supplementing in many places by children's bands and boys' clubs. Missions should be presented more systematically and effectively in the meetings of young people's societies, in guilds for young women and brotherhoods for young men. Of most strategic importance is the work in the colleges. In spite of the distractions of college life, which often absorb more time than the overcrowded curriculum, there is still time for mission study. We cannot assent to the name of a liberal education for one which omits the largest and most complex issue before Christendom to-day. We must press mission study in the colleges. But in this, even more than in the other lines, the quality of our work is supremely important.

All that precedes will be ineffectual if we do not succeed in training a special body of missionary teachers and workers. The demands indicated above cannot be adequately met by the pastorate, nor by our present force of interested laymen. There must be an increase in the number of workers who will be enthusiastic students of both missions and pedagogy, whose center of interest will not be in merely holding meetings but in achieving definite results. The mission study class will be one of the main agencies for securing such persons, and to secure this in turn we must have many more delegates at the normal classes of the summer conferences. In every local congregation there should be at least one such dynamo generating intense missionary enthusiasm, creating clear and deep convictions in those who are to be the lay leaders of the church. From the members of the study classes there should come an increasing number of candidates for the mission field. Missionary intelligence will be best assimilated by active discussion, rather than by silent listening. More important still is the providing an outlet in some form of active service. Impressions that fail to effect action cheat both the personal character and the cause. Missionary intelligence is not a mere chemical fertilizer, yielding inevitable increase when spread thickly over the soil. It is the appeal of God to the individual soul and to His Church, an appeal that needs the most careful adaptation to types and aims, an appeal that may even then be disregarded without the co-operative working of the Spirit of God.

The most crucial problem of foreign missions is, How to lead Christians to use what Dr. Arthur H. Smith, of China, has characterized as " The deeply buried talent of intercessory prayer." Without doubt the flood tide of superhuman power is held back from the missionary movement owing more largely to this cause than to any other. The evangelization of the world is not primarily a matter of numbers, wealth, knowledge, and strategy, but of the unhindered working of the Spirit of God. Such divine manifestation has been associated invariably with prayer. Whatever, therefore, influences Christians one by one and also corporately to devote themselves in the right spirit and manner to missionary intercession will most directly and effectively ensure the realization of the missionary purpose of Christ.

How to enlist the co-operation of Christians in prayer and how to increase their efficiency in this form of spiritual work is a most vital question. Mr. F. S. Brockman, the leader of the Student Movement in China, has well called attention to a great weakness in

this respect: " This promotion of a large volume of
prayer for the world's evangelization is thoroughly
practical. The great body of Christians have not hitherto taken seriously the efforts of leaders of missionary
work to promote prayer. This is due, no doubt, to the
fact that the leaders themselves have not seemed to
put prayer first. The burden of their appeal is for men
and money. The appeal for prayer is spasmodic and
incidental. If the same energy, time, earnestness, and
skill were put into getting prayer as are given to enlisting men and money, and if equally practical schemes
were devised for awakening the conscience of the
Church and for promoting the habit of daily prayer
for the world's evangelization, the Church would do
much to open the channels and let flow out the mighty
power of the Spirit of God which is necessary for
convincing and convicting the world."

If Christians are to be influenced to devote themselves more faithfully to prayer they must first be led
to realize deeply the possibilities of prayer and the
great need of their help in prayer. Professor War-
neck of Halle has shown that " It is much more difficult to pray for missions than to give to them. We
can only really pray for missions if we habitually lead
a life of prayer, and a life of prayer can only be led
if we have entered into a life of communion with God."
The promotion, therefore, of those practices and habits
which develop spiritual life and faith will indirectly
but powerfully help in developing and maintaining a
genuine prayer life. The reverent use of prayer
cycles and other aids to intercession which have been

developed within the Church during the centuries should be encouraged. Gatherings for united intercession, when properly prepared for and conducted, may serve as training schools in prayer and thus help to make more vital and fruitful the practice of private intercession. There is great need of more Christians becoming students in prayer. That it requires continued study, diligent and earnest practice, and resolute perseverance is well emphasized by the Commission on the Home Base in their Report to the Edinburgh Conference:

" It is not sufficient in an hour of vision and aspiration to dedicate ourselves to the work of intercession. Prayer is the putting forth of vital energy. It is the highest effort of which the human spirit is capable. Proficiency and power in prayer cannot be attained without patient continuance and much practice. The primary need is . . . that individual Christians should *learn* to pray. If this work is to be taken seriously, the hour of prayer must be definitely set apart and jealously guarded, in spite of weariness and many distractions. The secret and art of prayer can only be learned from the teaching of the Master Himself."

It need only be added that Christians learn to pray not only from the teaching of Christ but possibly even more from His contagious example. The more fully His life of unbroken communion, as well as His going apart for special intercession and His agonizing in the Garden on behalf of the world, are studied, the more deeply will the Church enter into the secret of overcoming the world. " Our duty to our generation involves a sense of spiritual responsibility that will open a Gethsemane wherever there is a Christian."

The state of the Church in Christian lands has a profound influence on the evangelization of non-Christian lands. The missionary enterprise is the projection abroad of the Church at home. It shares in a much larger measure than is usually recognized the ideals and spirit of the home Church, and carries their influence into the life of the Church which it creates in the non-Christian world.

This relation between the Church at home and the Church abroad has become increasingly close with the constant shrinkage of the world during the past few decades. As a result of improved means of communication the world has within a generation become one-third its former size. Nations which were as far apart as if they had been on different planets, so far as exerting a practical influence upon each other was concerned, have been drawn together, and the whole world, by means of the various applications of steam and electricity, has for the first time become one neighborhood. The nations and peoples have been drawn into closer touch with each other through trade and commerce, through the growing volume of travel, through the migration of students from land to land, through the influence of international societies of various kinds, through the activity of the press, through the development of international law, as well as through foreign missions. Moreover, some of the great nations of the West have acquired foothold, not only in Africa but also in the Far East. On account of the stupendous economic and social changes now taking place in the non-Christian nations, creating wants which at present can be supplied only by the West, these nations are entering into commercial relations with the West as never before. As a result of all this intermingling, the nations and races are acting and reacting upon each other with increasing directness, constancy, and power. No longer does the world exist in water-tight compartments. It is not strange, therefore, that the state of the home Church and its attitude toward the commercial, social, and political practices which obtain in so-called Christian lands should affect in a most real and vital way the progress and standards of the Church in the non-Christian countries.

Wherein does the state of the home Church affect the work of making Christ known to the non-Christian world? Manifestly it does so through its influence on the missionaries whom it sends forth. It is the home in which are enlisted and trained the pioneers, founders, and leaders of world evangelization. Much depends upon the environment or atmosphere in which they form their ideals and habits and receive their training. The missionaries, it is true, constitute an exceptional body of workers. In doctrinal integrity, ethical standards, and evangelistic zeal they are on a level which is not generally attained by the members of the home Church. This might be expected, since they constitute a very carefully selected company, and also from the fact that contact with the deep needs of the non-Christian world drives them back to fundamental realities. Yet the missionaries, consciously or

unconsciously, are deeply influenced by the home
Church. If its spiritual life is warm and vigorous,
this necessarily is a source of strength and inspiration
to them; whereas if the home Church is formal and
inert, it produces upon them a depressing effect. The
examples are not few showing that the theological unrest of the Church in certain Christian lands is re-
flected in the substance or spirit of the teaching by the
missionaries abroad. Moreover, the spiritual power of
the missionaries and their success in the work are
critically related to the measure and the fervor of
prayer on their behalf in the home Church.

The state of the home Church affects the work
through its influence on many of the native Christian
workers and members. Besides the influence com-
municated indirectly through the missionaries, an increasing number of native leaders study or travel in
Christian lands, read the periodicals and other literature of the West, and are thus more directly exposed
to the currents of thought in the home Church. One
does not need to look far to observe the influence of
the rationalistic spirit on Christian writers, teachers,
and preachers in Japan and India. With the increasing nearness of Christian and non-Christian lands, and
the multiplication of channels of intercourse between
them, the tendency will be for the Church, in the lands
to which the missionaries are sent, to adopt the religious standards of the lands which send them.

The state of the home Church affects the work by
the measure in which it is able to Christianize the
various influences through which Christian lands

affect non-Christian nations. Were the Church true
to its high calling, not only its professed members, but
the other people of Christian lands, would be more
thoroughly leavened by the ideals and motives of
Christianity, and the political actions of Christian nations would be more definitely governed by its principles. Thus the influences which go out from Christian lands along other than missionary lines would be
rendered helpful to the missionary enterprise. Un-
happily, the nominal Christianity, which in some cases
is virtual paganism, of some who represent Western
nations abroad in commercial and other pursuits is an
immense hindrance to the cause of Christ. The unchristian attitude of so many European and American
travelers towards the people of the lands which they
visit still further handicaps the success of mission
work. It would be difficult also to exaggerate the
evil effect produced by unrighteous aggressions on the
part of Western nations upon non-Christian nations
and peoples. Wrongly or otherwise, all these things
are often held up as proofs of the powerlessness of
the Christian religion.

Moreover, students and others who go from non-
Christian lands to study in the West, in many cases,
on their return to their homes, oppose Christianity because of the unchristian treatment which they have
experienced, or because of the anomalies and incon-
sistencies between the creed or ideals and the actual
conduct of Christians, as observed by them. They
are impressed by the fact that in nearly every Christian
land there are so many people outside the Church. A

Church too weak in faith and too lukewarm in spirit to fulfill its mission at home is thereby generating serious hindrances to the progress of its work abroad.

But most of all does the state of the home Church affect the work of the Church on the mission field through the direct and vital connection subsisting between the performance of this work and the quality and fulness of its own spiritual life. The work of making Christ known to the non-Christian world is rooted in the deepest motives of the Christian life; its imperative obligation is realized through a clear vision of the supreme truths of the Gospel; it demands consecration of lives and of substance in steadfast obedience to the divine call; it is a work imposed upon the whole membership of the Church, and, as the direct effort of the Church to fulfill the great task committed to it, it demands the consecration of all the available energies and resources of the Church for its thorough accomplishment. But the Church of to-day is very far from such a conception of its relation to the work of evangelizing the world. The spiritual life found in it is limited by want of enlightenment and by the imperfection of its communion with God. The growing spirit of commercialism and materialism which characterizes this age has cast its influence over the Church. It has promoted habits of luxury, softness, and worldliness, and manifests itself also in a lack of the sacrificial spirit. The attitude of the Church toward great social and national evils and sins is not suggestive of earnest purpose or adequate power to overcome them. It is a time of doubt and hesitation among many Christian ministers and teachers. Ultimate authority in religion is a subject of most diverse opinions. Cardinal doctrines are discussed as open questions. Whenever religion is thus thrown into the melting-pot, as it were, it is obviously enfeebled, for the time, in its propagating power. The life of the Church suffers from lack of clear conviction and of resolute loyalty to Christ throughout the whole sphere of duty. While the missionary obligation of the Church may be formally acknowledged, it is viewed with widespread apathy and indifference.

The consideration of the defects, shortcomings, and weaknesses of the home Church has led some to question whether we have a Christianity which should be propagated all over the world. Were it necessary to propagate the blemishes and errors of our Western Christianity this question would be most serious. Certainly we must exercise all vigilance not to dispense poison with the bread of life. We should avoid spreading errors which would neutralize the Gospel as it is presented in non-Christian lands. We must not press upon other races undesirable and unessential features of our Western Church life. Our Western idiosyncrasies of thought and practice and our endless sectarian subdivisions should be overcome or at least be left at home. Without doubt our home divisions are a great hindrance to the evangelization of the world. To the Oriental mind, for example, our denominational distinctions and varieties of emphasis are bewildering. Mozoomdar thus voiced this feeling: " You urge me to become a Christian. Which of the numberless forms of Christianity shall I accept? I shall always be a Christman, but never a Christian."

Happily the home Church still possesses the essentials of primitive Christianity. It sends forth its representatives to propagate the Christianity of the New Testament—to bring the non-Christian world face to face with the historic and the living Christ and with the teachings of His apostles. This is the Christianity that not only teaches God truly but gives God actually to the world, through His incarnation in Jesus Christ; and gives the world to God through its regeneration in Christ, by participation in His Spirit and Life. It is on this platform that all the victories of the Christian faith have been won. The worth of Christianity as a missionary force is measured by what it has of Christ. If He be lifted up He draws unto Himself men of all nations, races, and stations. The Church is more fully acquainted with Christ to-day than in any preceding age. Thus, though certain forms of our Christianity may not be worth propagating, our Christ should be proclaimed to all men. If we give to the world our best we shall be giving something that is infinitely worthy to be received by the world, and which also may justly claim the allegiance of the world. It is the only Christianity we have, and the only Christianity for the world. We cannot bring ourselves to consent to the proposition that it should not be propagated. In that wonderful letter which Dr. Rainy wrote on behalf of the Free Church of Scotland, in reply to the greeting of old Madras College students to the General Assembly in

Edinburgh on the occasion of Principal Miller's Moderatorship, the heart of the matter is aptly expressed: "We men in the West have no better claim to Jesus Christ than you have. We possess nothing so precious—we value nothing so much—we have no source of good so full, fruitful, and enduring—we have nothing to compare with the Lord Jesus Christ. To Him we bear witness. And we should gladly consent that you should cease to listen to us, if you would be led to give your ear and your heart to Him." Where this conviction and this spirit dominate the life of the Church, it possesses the vital force of missionary effort and sacrifice.

It thus appears that an essential part of the task of evangelizing the world is the lifting of the Church at home into a fuller spiritual life. As it learns the mind and heart of Christ, and is possessed by His Spirit, it will become more missionary, and also mightier in all its missionary work. In all planning for forward movements or for expansion of missions, this truth must be kept in the foreground. While it is true that a deepening interest in foreign missions invariably strengthens the spiritual life of the Church and promotes its fruitfulness in all directions, it is equally true that larger operations and greater power abroad are impossible unless the life of the Church at home is marked by greater enlightenment, devotion, and fidelity to its Lord. The two go together. The great need is that Christians young and old be given the vision, the motives, the enthusiasm which shall make the Church equal in spiritual power to the present world situation.

And this means that each Christian should in the most personal and practical manner strive to conform his life and practices to the requirements of his divine Lord and throw himself with great earnestness into the work of carrying out the missionary desires and purposes of Christ. Nothing less than a Church whose individual members are tremendously in earnest can evangelize the non-Christian world.

THE REQUIREMENTS OF
THE PRESENT SITUATION:
AN EFFICIENT CHURCH ON THE
MISSION FIELD

CHAPTER VI

THE REQUIREMENTS OF THE PRESENT SITUATION: AN EFFICIENT CHURCH ON THE MISSION FIELD

THE present situation on the mission field requires something more than an adequate plan of campaign and an adequate home base for missionary operations. There is even greater need of an efficient Church on the mission field. Even if the home Church were thoroughly alive to the situation and thoroughly inspired with the spirit of service, of itself it could not carry the Gospel to all men. The evangelization of the non-Christian world is not alone a European and a North American enterprise; it is to an even greater degree an Asiatic, an African, and a South American enterprise. While the Churches of Christian lands are responsible for the introduction of Christianity to non-Christian nations and for making sure that it is securely established in them, the principal burden of responsibility for the extension of Christ's Kingdom through each country rests upon the Christian sons and daughters of the soil. It was the opinion of that great missionary statesman, Alexander Duff, that "when the set time arrives, the real reformers of Hindustan will be well-qualified Hindus." Mackay of Uganda maintained that the agency by which and probably by which alone we can Christianize Africa is the African himself. Dr. Nevius, who had extensive experience in developing the native Church in China, expressed the conviction that the millions of China must be brought to Christ by Chinese. Practically all missionaries feel the same, and the reasons for their conviction are not difficult to find.

The task of making Christ known to all people is so vast that the number of foreign missionaries now on the field, or of those whom the home Church may reasonably be expected to provide, could not accomplish the work, even if they possessed the necessary qualifications and advantages. To evangelize China, for example, the number of foreign missionaries would need to be increased a hundred-fold. Again, even if the home Church could send out and support such an army of missionaries, the national spirit of the different non-Christian countries would make it impracticable for them to gain entrance. Unless the responsibility be recognized and accepted by the Christians of each mission field, it is hopeless to expect to see that field thoroughly evangelized and Christianized.

As a matter of fact native Christians possess marked advantages over foreign workers as evangelists. They do not have the disability of working in a climate to which they are not accustomed and which is unfavorable to them; they do not have to take furloughs or spend so much time at vacation resorts; while, on the other hand, in most mission fields, the problem of the climate is a very serious one for the foreign missionary, often resulting in breakdown of health, and always necessitating interruptions of the work by annual vacations, and frequent furloughs in the home-land. The native workers know the language of their people far better than most missionaries can ever hope to acquire it. Their intimate knowledge of its idioms and most telling expressions enables them to touch more readily and deeply the minds and hearts of their countrymen. Seldom does the missionary acquire the freedom, fluency, and accent so necessary for effective appeal. The native of the country understands the heart-life and the thought-life of his people. He is thus able to appreciate their feelings and point of view to a degree which the foreigner cannot attain. His familiarity with the superstitions, prejudices, and aspirations of the people is likewise a great advantage. Having fought over the battleground of the temptations of his own people, he is able to enter more sympathetically and helpfully into their experiences. He knows their soul struggles, their gropings after light, the trials incident to coming out from the social and religious associations connected with their family and community life. All of these things enable him to persuade and guide them better than can the missionary, who comes among them from entirely different surroundings and experiences, and who at the best is a stranger and a foreigner, in spite of anything he may do, and is therefore kept more or less aloof from the social as well as the spiritual life of the people whom he would help. The native Christians are thus qualified to be more efficient missionaries than the foreigners and for this reason, if for no other, it is clear that they must constitute the principal factor in spreading the Christian religion throughout their country.

Notwithstanding the fact that the major responsibility rests upon the native Christian workers, the co-operation of the missionaries in every mission field is still indispensable. They are needed to place at the disposal of the young Churches the experience and lessons of Christianity acquired through the many centuries of its history. They are needed to anchor and steady the Church on the mission field in times of stress and strain when there is serious danger of its slipping from its moorings in matters of doctrine and practice. There are sad chapters in the life of some of the native Churches which tell of the introduction into the life and teaching of the Church of ideas and practices of heathenism. Some thoughtful students of missions regard this as still one of the greatest perils on certain mission fields. Missionaries of the highest qualifications are needed on every mission field to present in their lives and work models and examples to the workers and members of the native Churches, and especially to communicate and to stimulate an aggressive evangelistic spirit. In the early stages of the development of the Church on every field, even in the later stages on some fields, the wise and loving co-operation of the missionary in the work of the Church is considered essential by most missionaries.

The missionaries are, moreover, imperatively needed to help to pioneer the work in the totally or largely unoccupied fields. A careful study of the world field shows that there is practically no non-Christian nation where their help as pioneers is not still needed. Upon this point Bishop Oldham has truly remarked: " When one considers the overwhelming preponderance of the non-Christians, the poverty of the native Christian Church, derived, as it is, after New Testament prec- edent, from the poor, the comparatively feeble mis- sionary pulse that as yet beats in it, it would be a betrayal of the non-Christians to leave them to a large extent to the missionary zeal of their native Chris- tian neighbors."

To leave the whole, or the major part of the evan- gelization of neighboring fields to the small, poor, and as yet narrow-horizoned Churches recently redeemed from the chill of heathenism, would be to sacrifice the many unevangelized for a doubtful experiment with the partially enlightened. It must be our object to throw the responsibility entirely upon the native Churches, as soon as they are ready to bear it. For the present it seems plain that both the initiative in entering new fields and the duty of securing and train- ing native preachers must lie largely with the foreign missionary.

Nevertheless, the great importance of the native Church as an evangelistic agency has already been proved. The history of the extension of Christianity, from the days of the early Church down to the present time, shows that the chief work of evangelizing and Christianizing a country has always been done by its inhabitants. Facts gathered from all the principal foreign mission fields show that this was never more true than it is to-day throughout the non-Christian world. Bishop Tucker, of Uganda, writes that " The work of winning the souls of the people of this country to Christ is really being done by the natives themselves, although under the supervision of foreign missionaries." Dr. Christie of Manchuria gives similar testimony: " Indeed, most of the converts have been brought in by one telling another what he had learned. There are several instances of a little Christian community being gathered in a new district wholly by the personal voluntary efforts of one native, who in some instances has not yet been baptized." Dr. John Ross stated at the Edinburgh Conference that probably less than one hundred of the 20,000 church members in Manchuria had been led to Christ solely by the missionaries. Dr. S. A. Moffett, of Korea, states: " The Korean Christians for the last ten years have been bringing in converts faster than the missionaries have been able to provide instruction for them."

The silent, constant, assimilating influence of the Church or the Christian community upon the surrounding population has been one of the most effective means of accomplishing this. The improvements in the individual and social life of the native Christians have been so evident and striking that they afford the most convincing evidence to non-Christian neighbors of the truth and power of Christianity. For example, the purer, happier, more unselfish, and more progressive home life of Christian families makes a silent, irresistible appeal. The non-Christians cannot but recognize the social, economic, intellectual, moral, and spiritual progress and transformations of their Christian neighbors as a result of Christianity, and they are thus convinced as by no other proof of its genuineness and claims.

The unconscious influence of one individual convert upon his associates has been another fruitful source of many additions to the Church. Quite apart from the direct, or technical preaching of the Gospel, one man, simply by breaking with the old religious system and becoming a Christian, influences another man to do so. This influence is brought to bear in many ways—through marriage, through the various relationships of communal life, through the personal regard of one man for another, through a father, mother, brother, sister, friend having taken the step, and, in India, through the relationship of caste. A Lutheran missionary estimates that in his mission, of the 15,000 and more baptized members, fully three-fourths were brought into the Church through one or the other of these different ways.

In all parts of the world, work by individuals to influence individuals to become Christians is the method most frequently and effectively employed. It seems to be of universal adaptation, but one receives the impression that it is more widely used by the Church on the mission field than by the Church in most of the Christian countries. The most striking example of fruitful personal work is given by Dr. Christie in the following narrative: " A patient came to the Moukden Hospital many years ago. When admitted, he had never heard the Gospel, but before he left he had a clear knowledge of Christian truth and showed an intense desire to make it known to others. For many years he witnessed for Christ, most of the time without salary of any kind, and under no control but that of his heavenly Master. The missionary who had charge of the district where he labored till his martyrdom by the Boxers, tells us that he was a direct means of leading at least two thousand souls into the fold of Christ." Dr. K. C. Chatterjee, one of the most distinguished Indian Christians, in showing how the Christians in the Punjab, both among the higher and lower classes, are animated by the spirit of spreading the Gospel, has testified that he himself was brought to Christ largely through the help and advice given to him by his Christian fellow-students. It is the general rule in Korea that the members of the Church engage zealously in personal work, and the method of house-to-house visitation is commonly practiced.

It is the custom in some fields to observe a Children's Day, when prayer is offered for the conversion of the youth of the community, when the teachers in the Sunday schools make special appeals, and when Christian parents put forth special efforts to lead their children to Christ. The results of this custom have been especially encouraging.

Preaching to their neighbors, or in near-by villages, by those who have become Christians is another fruitful method of extending Christ's Kingdom. It is quite common in Korea, in Manchuria, and in other parts of China for Christians to pledge to give a certain number of days to the work of public preaching, as well as to speaking to individuals one by one, subscribing their time just as Christians in the home lands promise their money. At one conference of Christians in Korea, after the members had adopted the tithe as the lowest standard of money-giving, they pledged enough time for evangelistic work to equal the time of one man for ten years. At another meeting one church member promised to devote to this kind of work without compensation during the following year one hundred and eighty days. In reporting at the annual meeting a year later he apologized because he had been able to give only one hundred and sixty-nine days. In Livingstonia it has become customary for large numbers of the church members to engage freely in preaching the Gospel. "Every Sabbath," says one at work in that field, "hundreds of our Christians preach in the villages around about their places. I fancy that from fifteen to twenty per cent. of the church members are engaged in teaching in Sabbath schools or in preaching every week, and that, entirely without pay. On Saturdays preachers' classes are held, when a sermon is suggested for the village preachers and a sermon outline given to them."

From many churches the Christians go out regularly in bands to evangelize neighboring towns and rural districts. This showing of the strength of their numbers seems to make a special impression. In connection with scores of mission colleges and schools it is quite common for bands of students to go out during their vacations on preaching tours. In the Tinnevelly district, where there are 95,000 Christians connected with the Anglican Church, almost every large congregation has its regular system of street preaching. During the past three or four years one large congregation in this district has set apart a special time each year when a large number of its members go out in bands to the neighboring villages to proclaim the Gospel. Last year as many as thirty bands witnessed for Christ among the villages within a radius of six miles. The plan of uniting all the Christians in a given town or district in a special evangelistic campaign, continuing through several days or even weeks, has been used with marked success in different fields. The most conspicuous examples are afforded by the Church in Japan, China, and India. Some of the largest and most difficult city fields of Japan have experienced remarkable revivals as a result of this method employed by the Japanese pastors and lay leaders, they themselves taking the initiative and bearing practically the entire burden of responsibility.

In addition to the increasing volume of evangelistic effort put forth by native Christians within the sphere of their daily callings and within the range of their immediate influence, a number of native churches and other groupings of native Christians in various fields are conducting organized missionary work to carry the Gospel to the unevangelized in distant regions of their own lands or of other and often remote countries. The West China Conference of the Methodist Episcopal Church in the Szechwan Province about three years ago organized an effort to send the Gospel to the

Tibetans. At a meeting of thirty of the Chinese ministers connected with this mission, where the needs of the Tibetans were brought to their attention, six ministers volunteered to work among these people at the gateway of Tibet. Two of their number were sent, and the Chinese Christians, under the leadership of their pastors, have continued to support these representatives. The presbytery of Korea, upon its recent organization, sent out one of its first seven ordained Korean ministers as a missionary to the island of Quelpart, the Korean Church providing his support and that of an evangelistic helper and of a Bible woman. The members of the Baptist Mission in Burma carry on an aggressive work, not only among the peoples of Burma but also among the Karens of Siam. Earnest native Christians have also gone out on their personal initiative to become missionaries among other tribes or races. The pioneer missionaries to Angoniland several years ago were Christian Kaffirs who went out from the Lovedale Institution in South Africa. A number of Hindustani Christians have gone to the Fiji Islands to do Christian work among the 35,000 Indians who have gone there to labor on the plantations, and these are supported in part by their fellow Indian Christians.

Special societies of native Christians have been organized for the express purpose of sending workers to distant parts. Almost every mission in South India now has a well-organized missionary society which sends missionaries to its own district and to some other part of its own country to work among people who speak different languages from their own; for example, the Home Missionary Society of the Madura Mission has taken the northern section of their district, an area covering 300 square miles, as its special field of work, and is supporting and directing six native Christian workers in that field. The Indian Missionary Society of Tinnevelly, organized in 1903, of Christians in the Tinnevelly district, now supports seven missionaries who are carrying on successful work in the Nizam's Dominions at a distance of over 800 miles from the home base. Besides supporting their own missionaries, this society maintains fourteen Telugu catechists, and has a number of other workers in special training. As a result of their labors there has been built up a community of two hundred baptized Christians and about 800 catechumens. The reflex influence has shown itself in greatly increased self-sacrifice, liberality, and prayerfulness in the home Church. In 1905 the National Missionary Society of India was organized with its fields of labor in the Montgomery district of the Punjab and in four other parts of India.

A missionary society was formed four years ago by members of the Manchurian Church to carry the Gospel to the outlying parts of Manchuria and the lands of Mongolia and Korea. Two workers at that time volunteered for service anywhere. The little congregations, out of their poverty, gave the first year $750 toward this movement. The two volunteers were ordained as pastors and sent to the capital of Halungkiang Province, several hundred miles north. There,

HON. T. H. YUN, OF KOREA   RAJAH SIR HARNAM SINGH, OF INDIA

Leading Oriental Laymen

in the face of hardship and difficulty, they have opened a chapel and are carrying on a vigorous propaganda. Chinese Christians, returning from California to the Kwangtung Province, were greatly distressed at the degradation and paganism of their unconverted relatives and neighbors. They were led to organize the Chinese Missionary Society of California, and as a result, within three years, four churches have been organized, and eight schools have been opened. The work is carried on without any foreign supervision, and is supported entirely by Chinese Christians. Japanese missionary societies have been formed to take the Gospel to the Japanese in Formosa, Korea, and Manchuria, and Korean associations have been organized to spread Christian truth among the Koreans in Manchuria, Siberia, Hawaii, and California.

The students and native teachers in some of the mission colleges of the Orient are also carrying on missionary work in distant lands. Possibly the best illustration is that of the Jaffna Students' Missionary Society, which maintains one of its graduates in evangelistic work among the Tamils of Southern India. These illustrations are typical of a widespread and growing missionary interest in the native Church. They afford ground for the impression which some travelers and students of missions have formed, that in point of evangelistic and missionary zeal the Church on the mission field compares favorably with that on the home field.

All this effort is full of promise for the future. It shows that the spirit of evangelism has taken root in

the native Churches, and that in them it is proving
itself capable of growth. But notwithstanding this
fact, it is true that in many places such a spirit is
almost, if not entirely, lacking, and even in the places
where the situation and outlook are most favorable
there is need of increasing the efficiency of the native
Church. This is not at all surprising when we reflect
upon the conditions. The larger part of the native
Church in Asia and Africa has been but comparatively
recently brought out of the selfishness of heathenism.
Moreover, heathenism and the social life have divided
the people largely into tribes, clans, castes, classes,
with much mutual help within these groups, but with
an instinctive drawing away from all others. The
missionary spirit of Christianity does tend to overcome
this repulsion and indifference to those outside, but it
is not without great difficulty and not without divine
assistance that Christians of the first generation overcome it and become filled with a passion for helpfulness. That so many have done so is a proof of the
reality of their Christianity, but that must not blind
us to the fact that a very large section of the native
churches has not advanced so far in the Christian life.
One of the most vital and pressing of all questions is:
How a still stronger evangelistic and missionary spirit
is to be developed in the churches on the various mission fields? If this could be accomplished a great step
would be taken towards the complete evangelization of
the world.

In order to do this, there must be, first of all, missionaries who are themselves filled with the evangelistic

spirit. If they obviously make their first business that of bringing others under the sway of Christ, their spirit is sure to become communicative. The missionary should not, however, rely merely upon the influence of his example; he must also keep urging upon the converts the privilege as well as the duty of seeking to influence their unconverted neighbors to become disciples of Christ. If the missionary is to do this in the face of all the difficulties which confront him, he must have a clear and mastering conviction that the most highly-multiplying work he can do is that of increasing the number of Christians filled with the desire to win others to Christ.   To lead a hundred Christians to become earnest soul winners is doubtless a more productive work than for one by himself to have preached throughout a large province, however desirable the latter work may be.

There is much to commend the practice which is followed by the American Presbyterian Mission in South China. The leaders of that mission consider that they cannot too strongly emphasize the duty of the saved to carry the Gospel to the unsaved, and are in the habit of asking converts at the time of their baptism if they are willing to work diligently for the salvation of others. This practice results in a constant stream of accessions to the Church. The Canadian Presbyterian Mission in Honan has the same policy, but has carried it even further. So fully have they accepted the practice of leading others to Christ as a necessary mark of genuineness on the part of the convert, that, as a mission, they have decided not to baptize any person unless he has led some one to Christ. The obligation to lead others into the Christian life should, however, be urged upon the members of the Church, not only at conversion but constantly. In those missions which are most fruitful in evangelistic results the leaders lose no opportunity of doing this, and doubtless one reason why so many native Christians in other missions are not actively engaged in this kind of service is simply that they have not been so carefully taught their duty and the terrible need of people without Christ. Wherever Christians are led to have a realizing sense of the condition of the people without the Gospel, and to see that their personal efforts are indispensable to meet the need, they are much more likely to give themselves to this unselfish ministry.

As a rule, however, it is necessary to do more than to present the facts of the obligation and need. In addition to pressing upon the native Christian his duty to evangelize his neighbors, it is important to assign some definite evangelistic task to him—something which in all probability will not be done unless he does it. His missionary zeal may be quickened and his efficiency may be increased by thus giving him a suitable part in the programme of extension. It will be of little value, however, to place such a burden upon him if he be not trusted with it and left to discover his own way of carrying it out. Otherwise he will not feel that the work is his own.

Missionaries have further enlisted native Christians in the work of evangelization by taking them on evangelistic tours. Dr. Mackay of Formosa was in the habit of taking a group of students with him when he went out to preach in the towns and villages, and Mr. Sherwood Eddy has followed the same method in much of his evangelistic work in the villages of Southern India. In this way those who accompany the missionary are especially influenced by the example of evangelistic zeal which he sets for them, and at the same time they receive invaluable instruction as to the manner and methods of presenting the Gospel and of conducting evangelistic services. The missionary activity of those who take part in these tours becomes much more vigorous and effective.

Conferences of Christians for the deepening of the spiritual life, which are now becoming quite as common on the mission field as on the home field, are of the very greatest value in developing the evangelistic spirit. By purifying and strengthening the native workers and uniting them in praying and planning they have exerted a powerful, indirect influence in kindling evangelistic fires in the communities to which the delegates have returned. The Sialkot Convention in the Punjab is one of the most famous of these gatherings. It had its origin in the daily prayer, for more than two years, of a group of four or five men, and to-day large numbers of missionaries, Indian ministers, lay workers, and church members from missions near and far meet together for prayer, instruction, exhortation, and praise. During each of the days of the convention continuous prayer is offered during the whole twenty-four hours. Marvelous outpourings of the Holy Spirit have been manifested; men have been led to confess their sins and to make restitution for wrongs. A passion to win men to Christ has resulted, and also a desire on the part of the native Christians to attain self-support for their churches. Conferences of this nature, if developed and wisely guided, will do much to cultivate within the Church the spirit of consecration and loyalty to Christ, which must result in the effort to extend His Kingdom.

A native Church cannot, however, become efficient as an evangelizing agency unless it be ably led. Perhaps the greatest need, therefore, of the native Church is that of multiplying the number of well-qualified native ministers and Christian workers. The idea of carrying the Gospel to the whole world or to any one of the great non-Christian nations in our day, apart from the raising up of an army of suitable native ministers and other Christian leaders, is not likely to be realized. Undoubtedly several thousands of the choicest spirits, which the universities and colleges of the United States, Canada, Great Britain, Australasia, Germany, and other Christian lands can furnish, will be required to pioneer the work in non-Christian lands, to plant the Church, to guide the Church in the midst of special trials, and, above all, to train a native leadership; but for every hundred missionaries there will be needed thousands of native workers to serve as pastors, teachers, evangelists, catechists, and Bible women. The necessity for a thoroughly trained native agency has been recognized by the great missionary statesmen. Joseph Neesima, the eminent Japanese Christian educator, after years of Christian work in Japan, said that

BISHOP HONDA, OF JAPAN

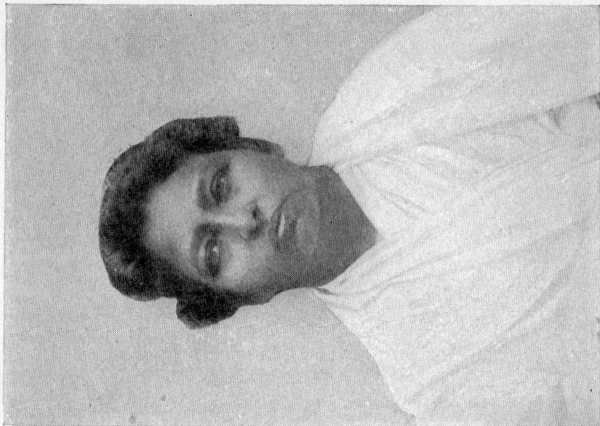

PANDITA RAMABAI, OF INDIA

the best possible method to evangelize her people is to raise up a native force. Dr. Goodrich of North China urges that whether this question be viewed economically, politically, historically, or sociologically, the only sound method of evangelizing a great nation is that of raising up and using a qualified native agency. This is the need of the native Church, therefore, on which the missionaries should concentrate their attention.

There are very serious difficulties to be overcome before this need can be met. In most non-Christian countries religious workers are held in contempt. This is unlike what one usually finds in the United States and Canada and in other Western lands, where the Christian ministry has dignity and prestige as a result of its honorable position and influence for centuries. Throughout Asia to-day, largely as a result of the corrupt lives of many of the priests, the religious callings are looked down upon, if not despised. Unwillingness to incur the reproach which often attaches to the native worker who is related to the foreigner, is another difficulty which keeps many from entering Christian service as a life-work. They do not like to be called foreign hirelings, as a Japanese expressed it; or, as a Chinese put it, they do not want to be twitted with eating the foreigner's rice. There is also the question of status which seems to stand in the way of some in India and other lands. That is, the native workers feel that they are entitled to more power, liberty, and responsibility than they have, that they should receive larger recognition, that more confidence should be shown in them by the missionaries. In some cases they have good reasons for this opinion, but doubtless in more cases their attitude is due to a misconception of the motives and spirit of the missionaries. Nevertheless, this is a very real difficulty and it is not easily overcome.

The opposition of parents and relatives is a very great hindrance to securing native Christians of ability for the ministry. In countries where the Confucian ethics dominate, or where the system of caste exists, or in parts of the world like Africa where there are strong tribal bonds, it is exceedingly difficult for young men to enter Christian callings in the face of the expressed objection of parents, relatives, and friends. The attractions presented by commercial pursuits, by government service, and by other so-called secular walks of life, is a prominent reason, if not the principal one, why it is so difficult to-day to get a sufficient number of able native students to devote their lives to Christian work. The salaries paid in the secular callings range all the way from a little larger to thirty or more times greater than is paid in Christian service. It is just as if the students of the United States and Canada were offered salaries of $5,000 to $10,000 to enter certain business, professional, or political positions. If this were done, it would greatly increase the difficulty of inducing a sufficient number of men to enter the Christian ministry at home.

A lack of spirituality is perhaps the most serious of all the causes making it difficult to get a sufficient number of able native leaders for Christian work. In non-Christian lands there are many young men who have a hold upon Christianity, but upon whom Christianity does not have a powerful hold. Wherever one finds native Christians upon whom the Spirit of God has laid His mighty hand, one finds men eager to enter upon the service of their fellow-men and therefore willing to face the hardships, opposition, and sacrifices involved.

The lack of adequate efforts and measures to discover and enlist more workers of the right qualifications is one of the most fundamental reasons why they are not forthcoming. Societies which have given most attention to this problem are the ones which have succeeded in raising up the largest number of effective leaders. The missionaries who desire most earnestly to be used by God in enlisting young men and young women for this all-important service and who have given time to this work are those who are turning the largest number of young men and young women into Christian work as a life-work.

What can be done to meet the difficulties to which attention has been called and to raise up the army of native Christian workers who will lead the forces of the Church on the mission field to accomplish the evangelization of the non-Christian world? It is necessary greatly to enlarge and to strengthen the educational missionary work. While there is need of improving the material equipment of mission schools and colleges there is even greater need of adding to the force of educational missionaries. At present this part of the foreign staff is far too small. It is poor economy to erect large educational plants and leave them under-manned to such a degree that they fall short of being productive investments. The workers in many cases are so overburdened with the technical work of teaching, which ought, for the honor of the Church, to be kept up to scholarly standards, that they are not able to give the time that they so much desire to devote to the most vital part of all, influencing deeply the faith, the character, and the life plans of the students. The staff in every place, where necessary, should be increased to such an extent that each educational missionary will have time to do personal work and to pray with the students. In choosing educational missionaries particular care should be exercised to select those who, in addition to their scholastic attainments and their high qualifications as educationists, are also dominated by the desire and purpose to influence their students to become Christians and to devote their lives to Christian service. The Presbyterian College, established by Dr. and Mrs. Calvin Mateer in the Shantung Province of China, has throughout its history yielded a remarkably large proportion of its strongest students for the service of the Church. The main reason for founding the college was that it might raise up and train a native ministry, and the main energies of the educational missionaries were expended in this direction. Dr. Mateer seldom uttered a prayer but the burden was that God would raise up men to be pastors and leaders of the Church. The students knew that Pastor Ding, who has recently been so greatly used in promoting spiritual awakenings among students in China, had the same wish, and in going to him, as invited, for conversation, went armed with reasons why it was absolutely impossible for them to be ministers. But Ding never mentioned the subject to them, but went to God in private. The result was that after a while the students thronged his room, with the same difficulties, but urging him to pray that these might be removed and recording the purpose to enter the ministry. Scores of them decided to enter this calling.

The Student Young Men's and Young Women's Christian Association movements and other societies of Christian students in the non-Christian world can also help greatly in the work of recruiting the ranks of Christian workers. In fact, these societies were established by the missionaries or at the call of the missionaries for the express purpose of helping the Church to evangelize students and to influence them to devote their lives to Christian service. In a true sense they constitute a student volunteer movement for home missions. The methods employed by them are such as have been most fruitful in the student communities of the West. The devotional, constructive study of the Bible is much emphasized. There are to-day over 5,000 native Christian students engaged in the Bible classes of these Associations. Among other methods used are personal work, evangelistic campaigns in the neighborhood and during vacations in more remote districts, and the development of study of the work of the Church. Greater stress should be laid by all these societies on influencing the strongest students to devote themselves to Christian work as a life-work. Visits should be made more frequently by secretaries to the mission colleges with this one end in view. In each of a number of these Associations within the past few years, such as at Peking University, Shantung Union College, and the College at Assiut, Egypt, between one and two hundred students have been led to dedicate their lives to Christian service. Were special efforts made, similar results might be forthcoming in many other mission schools. The Associations in the government colleges are also helping to secure recruits for the Christian ministry. No graduates of the Imperial University of Japan had ever entered the ministry until the Association had been at work for some years, but now three graduates are in the ministry and several others are preparing for this calling.

An important means of securing and developing able native leaders of the Church is to give men of ability places of real leadership. Leaders can never be developed except through bearing responsibility. The foreign missionary must, therefore, more and more recognize that the work on the mission field is primarily that of the native leader and minister and not that of the foreign missionary with the native as helper. The missionary must have the spirit of John the Baptist and, in loving humility, must be willing to decrease that the native worker may increase in ability, fruitfulness, and position. The efficient native Church will not have fully come until its full leadership is in the hands of native Christians. The wise missionary

THE MADRAS CHRISTIAN COLLEGE

will work and pray and place himself in the background that this may be accomplished at the earliest possible moment. He will rejoice when the initiative is taken by the native ministers and workers rather than by himself, and will be pleased with the more obscure position of sympathetic counselor and friend rather than that of the authoritative leader of the Church.

One of the deepest secrets of enlisting an adequate number of leaders of the native Church, possessed with the evangelistic spirit, is the development of the spiritual life of the native Church. Out of such a Church will come men who are willing to offer themselves for Christian service in the face of all the difficulties which they meet. It is, therefore, of the utmost importance that methods be employed to build up the faith and character of the native Christians and to lead them to yield themselves wholly to the sway of Christ and His Spirit.

Above all there is need for far more intercession for the raising up and thrusting forth of this army of native leaders. This is necessary in order to make all the other means truly effective and most largely productive. It is the only means on which Christ has placed stress in connection with solving the problem of securing workers. Any method, therefore, which neglects this point is superficial. The Church should not leave unappropriated and unapplied this great force for the raising up and enlisting of laborers. Moreover, it is a means which is available to the humblest and most obscure Christian, both at home and on the mission field.   It is, therefore, possible for each Christian to be mightily used in helping to solve the problem of securing an efficient Church on the mission field by using the divinely appointed and all-prevailing method commanded by Christ.

THE REQUIREMENTS OF THE PRESENT SITUATION: THE SUPERHUMAN FACTOR

CHAPTER VII

THE REQUIREMENTS OF THE PRESENT SITUATION: THE SUPERHUMAN FACTOR

As one surveys the enormous task involved in making Christ known to all the world, and realizes the inadequacy of human agents and agencies as well as of human policy and strategy, the first impression is that the Church is totally unable to discharge its overwhelming responsibility. The next and dominant impression is that Almighty God is able, and that the Church must be led to avail itself of His limitless resources to a degree hitherto unknown since that vital age—the first generation of Christianity. Missionaries, native Christian workers, and leaders of the missionary activities on the home field, while they differ on nearly all questions pertaining to plans, means, and methods, are absolutely united in the conviction that the world's evangelization is a divine enterprise, that the Spirit of God is the great Missioner, and that only as He dominates the work and workers can we hope for success in the undertaking to carry the knowledge of Christ to all people. They believe that He gave the missionary impulse to the early Church, and that to-day all true mission work must be inaugurated, directed, and sustained by Him.

No lesson of missionary experience has been more fully, impressively, and convincingly taught than that, apart from the divine working, all is inadequate. The hope and guarantee of carrying the Gospel to all the non-Christian world do not rest principally on external favoring advantages which Christianity may possess in certain fields; nor upon the character and progress of the civilization of Christian countries; nor upon the number, strength, experience, and administrative ability of the missionary societies; nor upon the variety and adaptability of missionary methods and the efficiency of missionary machinery; nor upon an army of missionary evangelists, preachers, teachers, doctors, and translators—much as these are needed; nor upon the relation of the money power to the plans of the Kingdom; nor upon aggressive, and ably led, forward missionary movements, either in the home Churches or on the foreign field—but upon the living God dominating, possessing, and using all these factors and influences.

Everything vital to the success of the movement to carry the Gospel to all the non-Christian world depends upon the power of God Himself. In His hands is the government of the world. He has intrusted enormous powers to Christian nations. His providence has opened the door to the non-Christian countries, determined the order of their occupation, and developed agencies and influences which facilitate the spread of Christianity.

Investigation has furnished countless illustrations, showing that God has preceded the messengers of the

Gospel, and prepared the people to understand it and to be responsive to it. The Spirit of God is working continuously in all parts of the world in the hearts of men, apart altogether from the main channel of His revelation, which culminated in Christ. Christian workers, therefore, should approach people with their message, recognizing that the Spirit has preceded them. This normal working of the Spirit universally in the human heart should be recognized, and every manifestation of His working should be welcomed, in the belief that " God is no respecter of persons but in every nation he that feareth him and worketh righteousness is acceptable to him." Unquestionably God had been working in the world through all the centuries before the coming of Christ. " My Father worketh even until now, and I work." He has been working through the non-Christian religions, not alone in using such truths as they may possess for the betterment of men, but also in making these religions a schoolmaster to lead the peoples to recognize in due time their need of Christ. The Rev. E. Allegret, a missionary of the French Congo, has thus described his experience, which is similar to that of many other missionaries in different parts of the world: " I have been witness to numerous genuine conversions followed by lives truly transformed, but that which has astonished me the most is, that time after time I have come among people who were expecting me and who were prepared to receive my Gospel message. One time a company of natives after a long march emerged from the great forest and arrived upon the banks of the river where they found us. They reported that they had wondered whether in following the sun they might not find God, and they indicated that it seemed quite natural that God should enable them to meet us and should thus answer their unconscious prayer."

It is God who chooses and thrusts forth the workers of His own appointment. The pages of missionary history teach no lesson with more abundant and satisfying illustrations. The leaders of the Church Missionary Society, of the China Inland Mission, and of other missionary organizations, have borne testimony to the fact, that again and again, when they have greatly needed missionary candidates but have been unable to secure them, and have made their need a subject of united intercession, invariably the new workers have been forthcoming. On the authority of Christ, it is hopeless to expect to secure a sufficient number of missionaries apart from His compelling power, and even were it possible, they would prove incompetent for the great work. Experience is showing that when chosen and dominated by His Spirit, a few men can do more than an army chosen only by men. It is He who communicates to the workers, both foreign and native, power not naturally their own, which qualifies them to do His work. He it is who guides workers as truly to-day as in New Testament times, to discover the lines along which the Kingdom is to be extended and built up. The large, growing, and permanent spiritual results are the product of His gracious and life-giving work. The secret of the power of those missionaries who accomplish the largest and deepest work is not what they do and say, but the presence of Christ in them, and with them. They see with His eyes, feel with His heart, work with His energies. Christ is everything with them. They move among men as embodiments of His superhuman power, under Whose vitalizing touch dead souls start into life. The power of God may be seen also in the ability given to His servants to go on working steadily year in and year out, even with little or no apparent results, but sustained by a sense of duty and by an undying hope that the Lord will surely see of the travail of His soul and be satisfied. Moreover, no one but the almighty Spirit can cause the missionaries of the different Christian communions, and also the native Christian workers, to work with that harmony and unity and spirit of true brotherhood which are essential to universal conquest.

God alone enables workers to face with calm and courageous hearts the stupendous obstacles and difficulties which lie across their path, and to triumph over them. The fearful inertia and conservatism of the non-Christian world; the prevalence of ignorance, superstition, falsehood, moral perversity and coarseness, fear, fatalism, godlessness, selfishness, and lovelessness; racial prejudice and antagonisms; the corrupt lives and practices of representatives of Christendom—all this would leave the workers discouraged and dismayed were it not for faith in the living Christ. Only the quickening powers of His Gospel can overthrow or transform systems of error rooted for thousands of years, and entwined with the laws, institutions, customs, and sentiments of peoples of ancient civilizations. The vast extent of the work to be done and the subtle and baffling obstacles which oppose, are such that nothing less than the action of the omnipotent God behind the presentation of the truth of Christ will enable it to prevail and overcome.

It is God who overrules occasions and events, human movements and powers, for the furtherance of the Gospel. Diplomacy has often been unfortunate; commerce has selfishly opposed the spread of Christianity; the prejudice of the officials and of the people has resisted the introduction of the Gospel. But all these, together with persecutions, wars, and national calamities, have been turned to the progress of the Gospel. Many have called attention to the overruling hand of God in connection with the Boxer uprising in China. They recognize His power and guidance in the fact that the very action which was intended to extirpate Christianity from China has had, as one of its results, an unprecedented forward movement in missionary work in that country, and that since the year 1900 the doors have been opened to the Gospel far wider than before. Dr. Ford of Syria says, " Rarely has the hand of God been more plainly revealed in the march of human events than it was in the crises of July, 1908 and April, 1909 in Turkey. These are indications of the revelation of the supernatural factor in advancing the Kingdom of God in the world."

Modern missions constantly confirm the fact so prone to be forgotten, that it is the Spirit of God Who alone has the power to convict men of sin. It is

only when He convicts of sin and of dire need that
the soul becomes willing to hear of Christ as a Saviour.
The genuine fruits of the Spirit, as shown in conviction, repentance, restitution, and the making up of
long-standing quarrels, have afforded convincing proof
that God alone brings home the Gospel with power to
the hearts and consciences of men. Even in discourag-
ing fields of China, He has shown His ability to overcome the fear of " loss of face," and to call forth
heartbreaking confessions—not of ordinary shortcomings and failures, but of sins which the Chinese would
endure anything in order to conceal. Men have been
moved to confession of sin through the working of this
unseen Agent in their lives, who could not be moved
by any human agency or influence. The Chinese are
naturally a stolid people, little given to emotion; but
workers state that such rending of the heart under
conviction of sin they have never seen in the home
lands. Bishop Warne gives this remarkable testimony :
" After twenty years of personal experience and close
observation, I can testify that, apart from the direct
work of the Holy Spirit in convicting non-Christians
of sin, I have never known the conversion of an individual to the real Christian life and experience.
Among a people whose consciences are educated in
the vagaries of the Vedantic philosophy of India,
which leaves the individual without a consciousness of
personal and moral responsibility, there is absolutely
no hope except in the awakening to, or the creating
of, a consciousness of sin and moral responsibility by
the direct work of the Spirit of God. I have seen

thousands of instances of awakening and transformations of character nothing short of the miraculous."

There can be no more marked and unmistakable proof of a present-day working of a superhuman power than the work of the Holy Spirit in such conversions as are taking place in increasing numbers from year to year in all parts of the non-Christian world. The breaking down, for example, of the pride of a Moslem until, conscious of his sin, he humbles himself at the Cross, and becomes a new man in Christ Jesus, is a contemporary evidence of the superhuman character of the Christian faith. The Rev. G. Raquette, of the Swedish Mission in Turkestan, gives an account of the conversion of a Mohammedan mullah: "He had tried for years in vain to fulfill the commandments of the Mohammedan religion. He saw only faults in himself and in his religion, and could find no light. At last he began quite secretly to think of Jesus Christ, whose name he had seen in the Koran. Something within him seemed to tell him that Jesus was the Prophet by whom he could find the way to God. But there were no Christians, no teachers, and no books to instruct him. Then he began to pray to God in the name of Christ. He kept up this practice every day for nine years, until one day he found a copy of the Gospels, and then found a great light and peace. He became exceedingly delighted and happy. He became baptized, and was the first Mohammedan of Bokhara to find Christ." The Rev. W. M. Beck, of the Lutheran Mission in Liberia, tells of the conversion of another Moslem: "One morning I met a mullah, and after some friendly conversation asked him to explain his doctrine, which he was glad to do at considerable length. Then I repeated to him the Gospel story and compared the leaders of the Christian and Mohammedan faiths and their doctrines. He was deeply impressed, and on parting remarked, ' If what you say is true, and I believe it is, I must quit teaching Mohammed and teach Jesus.' Some days later, when I met his son, he told me that his father had turned from teaching the Koran and was preaching Jesus."

The fact that men who were living indifferent, callous, degraded, sensual, proud, cruel lives have become pure, faithful, kind, spiritual, and zealous, and that they are triumphantly resisting their old temptations, is satisfying evidence that there is a power greater than human in the missionary movement. The story of " Old Wang," one of the first men baptized in the United Free Church Mission in Manchuria, has often been told. He was converted from being a selfish opium slave to an earnest Christian worker, who devoted his whole life to the well-being of others. His mother and his younger brother became Christian believers as a result of observing the mighty change in his own life. Dr. J. E. Walker, of Foochow, tells of another opium convert: " He was not a man of strong will and was a complete slave to the terrible opium habit, but through the prayers and faithful ministry of one of our preachers, he has been completely delivered. The almost universal testimony of physicians who have had to deal with such cases is that thorough enslavement to this habit is attended with a physical degeneracy and a weakening of the will which renders reform a physical or human impossibility." The Rev. O. Bodding, of Santalia, India, has written about the conversion of an honorary magistrate who was addicted to many of the heathen vices: " He had spoken very disdainfully to others, and had sworn that he would never become a Christian. Purposely I did not speak to him about Christ, and I forbade others to do so. Many had tried to influence him, but had been routed by him. I centered my hope in prayer on his behalf, and in the Word of God, in which I sought to interest him. We read together the book of Romans. It filled him with questionings. It was plain that the Spirit of God was working in his heart. After about four months he made up his mind and asked to be taken under instruction for baptism. He is now the leader of one of our congregations, and through the grace of God is a redeemed and cleansed character. He was gained solely through the influence of the Spirit working through the Scriptures." The Rev. F. J. F. Van Hasselt of Dutch New Guinea tells of the conversion of one of the fiercest opponents of Christianity. He says that he was " a drunkard, adulterer, robber, and murderer—one who, under a regular government, would have been a candidate for the scaffold. He called on me and asked to be baptized, being tired of sin. I could hardly trust my ears, as I had almost given him up as hopeless. After a time of probation he was baptized, and has ever since lived an exemplary life. He often accompanies me at his own request on evangelistic tours, and gives a powerful testimony. Although belonging to the higher class, he is not ashamed to repair my boat and serve me without accepting payment. In view of cases like this, one cannot doubt the personal working of the Holy Ghost."

Director P. A. Gericke, working on the island of Java, has thus told of the conversion of a Mohammedan village magistrate. "He stole money from the Government and ran away to another part of Java, where he settled down under a changed name. There he came in contact with Christians, attended the meetings, received baptismal instruction, and was later baptized. On account of his good conduct and his talents, one of our missionaries made him his helper. One day he came to the missionary and asked for his dismissal on the ground of unworthiness. As a reason he named the theft which he, as a magistrate, had committed years before. Although not compelled to do so, he gave himself up of his own accord to the police, because he felt that only in this way could he satisfy his conscience. The Dutch officials were profoundly impressed by his action. In the prison he preached Christ, and showed forth an attractive Christian life."

Nothing but the uplifted Christ, drawing men to Himself, will account for the noble and Christlike characters raised up on the mission fields from among those whose lives were degraded and whose natures were hardened and unresponsive. It is in Him they begin to see God, for He brings God near to them and reveals to them God's loving-kindness and saving power. In Him they see in human form and action the holiness, love, and power of the unseen God. One after another, men and women in middle and advanced life, as well as the young, give up their pride and sinful practices, and all that has made up the essence of their unholy life in the past, and then go out and testify by life and word among their neighbors that they have passed from darkness into light. The Rev. R. Fassmann, of German East Africa, tells of an aged woman named Mandoro, who in the course of instruction for baptism, in answer to his question whether there was a sinless human being on earth, replied that there was one, and on further questioning she mentioned the name of a Christian man in the community and told of his Christlike deeds. Missionaries who have observed these radical changes, and who have had opportunity to talk with such persons, to see the way in which the problems of life are faced by them from the Christian standpoint, to understand their motives and spirit, and to watch their consistent Christian lives, have no doubt whatever that God and not man is the prime mover in the missionary enterprise, and that Christ is the center and innermost working power in these transformations of men.

The Rev. W. L. Ferguson, of Madras, points out the impossibility of accounting for the marked changes in disposition and character which are taking place on the mission field, apart from the working of God Himself. " I am continually led to wonder at the way in which these people become Christians. Most of them are so densely ignorant that they fail to follow anything like abstract thinking or philosophy. I have often been in despair when I have tried to reason out a case with them, and I am certain that if I were to attempt to teach them logic I should utterly fail. And yet they grasp the Gospel message—enough of it to make salvation available. The great essentials get a grip on their minds and hearts. They forsake idolatry and heathen practices; they believe in God; they receive Christ as Saviour, believing that He died for their sins, arose again, and that He is now alive and able to save and to sympathize. This may be the full extent of their apprehension, but it works marvels in their lives. I have seen some real saints among them, men and women consistent and spiritual in life and mighty in prayer. Such transformations tell greatly in the communities where the lives are lived." It does not take many cases of this kind to create an over-whelming impression that the Lord Christ is present in this world to-day, as really as He was in the villages of Galilee.

Writing from Korea, the Rev. J. E. Adams voices the conviction expressed by scores of missionaries from nearly all quarters of the world: "I have experienced, tested, and proved the sufficiency of the Holy Spirit in the work of the conversion of men, so constantly and with such invariable results, that any question on the subject has long ceased to exist. It has become one of the assumed working postulates of life. No man living in the conditions in which I have lived, even with the most rudimentary instincts of scientific observation, could arrive at any other conviction than that the Gospel is the power of God." It is this ethical and spiritual Christianity which will conquer the non-Christian nations. A truly spiritual life, proved by its ethical results and triumphant power over temptation, can alone satisfy their deepest needs. Such conversion is not simply a change in name, opinion, or belief, but a new spiritual experience, a coming to know personally the living Christ.

The great spiritual awakenings and revivals in different parts of the non-Christian world are the result of the work of the Spirit of God. The Rev. J. Goforth gives the following account of one of the typical spiritual awakenings in China: " One of the most marked manifestations of power that I have seen among the heathen was at a great idolatrous fair where seventy-six Chinese and Canadian Christian workers were in attendance. One night I spoke on I Tim. 2: 1-7, with special emphasis on the Crucified. So many in the audience seemed to be moved that one of the Chinese workers exclaimed, ' These signs are like unto those when Peter preached.' At another preaching hall on the following night I was speaking on I Peter 2: 21-27, and again laid special emphasis on the Crucified, and almost the entire audience stood up, saying, ' We will follow this Saviour.' Some of the Chinese workers were amazed at the results. On finishing the address I left the meeting in charge of another and retired to an inner room for prayer. It was then that one of the workers remarked, ' He for Whom we have so often prayed is among us to-night of a certainty, but if we would retain His presence we must walk carefully.' Up to this time we had never heard such fervent

praying from Chinese lips. In connection with this
and the other missions there were always signs of
intense conviction. Men and women were broken
down, confessed their sins, made restitution, and
yielded themselves to God. The sense of God's presence was overwhelming and soon became unbearable.
Others, Chinese as well as foreigners, who have passed
through scenes of judgment, have afterwards carried
the fire to other centers where the same divine results
have followed." Dr. W. M. Morrison, a missionary in
the Belgian Congo thus describes a recent awakening in that region: "The power of the Spirit of God
was present in a marvelous manner. Confession was
made in public of sins which would be unmentionable
at home; fetishes were renounced and publicly burned
or otherwise destroyed; restitution was made of stolen
goods, gambling gains, and other riches received as
the hire of sin. Great sinners were saved; backsliders
were restored; and evangelists were sent forth to
preach. A few of the converts have slipped back, but
many of the fruits of the revival remain to this day.
Two things are especially notable about these awakenings; first, they always come in answer to earnest,
believing prayer, sometimes after long waiting; and,
secondly, they come in connection with the proclamation and teaching of the Word of God." Other recent
wonderful revivals in China, in Northern and Southern
India, in all parts of Korea, and the famous Taikyo
Dendo in Japan a few years ago, not to mention similar awakenings in other decades, are traced by the missionaries to the same divine source.

One of the unmistakable evidences of the work of the Spirit of God is to be found in the way in which Christians endure trial and persecution. For example, the most marked characteristic of the Chinese Christians is their steadfastness, their willingness to endure hardship and even death for the sake of Christ. There has never been a time in the history of missions in China when the profession of Christianity did not entail risk of persecution. Even before the year 1900, the blood of martyrs had been frequently shed in China, and in that year several thousands of Christians were slain in the Boxer uprising because they would not renounce their faith. The Church in Manchuria in particular has for several years been subjected to very severe trials. During the war between China and Japan it suffered much. During the Boxer uprising many of the Manchurian Christians were slain, and many more died of disease resulting from exposure when endeavoring to escape. Others suffered greatly in connection with the recent war between Japan and Russia. These various trials, however, served to prepare the way for the recent remarkable revival which has done so much to purify and strengthen the spirit of the Church.

The members of the Eastern and Protestant Christian Churches in Moslem lands have also undergone terrible trials and persecutions. In 1895 and 1896 twenty-two Protestant pastors and preachers in Armenia were slain, and in April, 1909, twenty-one Christian pastors in Cilicia met death at the hands of the cruel Moslems. During these massacres thousands of the church members also were killed. The more one reads of the fearful ordeals of blood and fire through which the Christians of the Turkish Empire have passed, the greater is the respect one has for those who through it all have held to the name of Christ.

The transformation of communities as well as of individuals is also indicative of the work of Christ as God. The testimony of Bishop Tucker as to the complete change in the social life and practices of the people in Uganda under the influence of the Gospel is a good illustration; also, through the work of the Livingstonia Mission, other African tribes have been just as wonderfully transformed. The case of the Wild 'Ngoni is one of the most remarkable. Thirty years ago they were a tribe of the very fiercest savages, and one of the most degraded of all. Cruelty, murder, and impurity abounded among them. The women were downtrodden and oppressed. For the very least offence any one might be put to death. "A woman carrying a pot of beer would be killed in broad daylight in order to get the beer and prevent detection. A scream would be heard in the evening, and on inquiring the cause one would be told that it was a worn-out slave who had been cast out for the hyenas to devour." The tribes around lived in constant terror of their raids, which were always accompanied by the most wanton bloodshed, for the 'Ngoni did not consider themselves men until they had shed blood. In 1882, the first missionary—a Kaffir evangelist—began to work among them, and very quickly a change was noticed. In less than ten years the war spirit was broken, and in twenty years it was entirely gone. The brutal raids upon the defenceless tribes had ceased, and slave-trading was impossible. To-day in many places the people gather night and morning to worship God, and there is a large and growing native Church. This transformation has taken place without the aid of any secular force and with the persistent savagery of the land as an opponent. Nothing but the power of God could have brought it to pass.

Another example is the marvelous uplifting of out-castes and lower castes in Northern and Southern India as a result of the power of the Gospel. The manner in which these most depressed and degraded of all the peoples in India have improved their social condition, rebuked and overcome the forces of vice, erected their own schools and churches, spread the Gospel among their neighbors, and suffered for Christ's sake, while leading quiet, consistent Christian lives, is truly wonderful. Dr. John Ross, of Manchuria, says that while "Education is good, and other intellectual and physical aids as well, all these combined and at their very best would never have evolved the Church in Manchuria from the mass of foreigner-hating idolaters who filled the land." Another remarkable example of the influence of the Gospel is seen among the Miao tribes of West China. Communities that less than a decade ago were ignorant, degraded, and very immoral are now Christian. The complete transformation of certain of the Pacific Islands constitutes another striking example. One does not find examples of such transformations of communities as a result of the teaching of the Baghavad Gita or the Ramayana or of the entrance of the Koran. It is the working of powers that transcend human explanations, accompanying the proclamation of the story of Christ and His Cross, that accomplishes these wonders.

Another evidence of God's power is seen in the way in which He fills the native Christian with a passion for helping others, especially those in deepest need. On all the mission fields there have been many splendid examples of new converts making sacrifices that they might tell others of the salvation which they had found. The manner in which many hundreds of the ablest young men of the different non-Christion nations and races have refused worldly advancement and devoted their lives, on comparatively insignificant salaries, to the work of evangelizing their non-Christian countrymen and of carrying the good tidings of salvation into regions beyond, is a striking manifestation of God's working. In fact, there is nothing more encouraging anywhere, and nothing which so clearly proves the reality of their Christian experience. The Bishop of Hankow maintains that " it is difficult, if not impossible, to account for so many Chinese Christian young men entering upon the arduous and comparatively poorly paid work of the ministry without ascribing it to the direct influence of the Holy Spirit. Most of them had to suffer serious persecution when they became Christians, and the older among them have shown by their lifelong devotion and steady growth in Christian character the manifold fruits of the Spirit." Bishop Warne gives an interesting illustration of the same point in writing of one of the Indian preachers: "He was in a theological school receiving ten rupees, and his wife was getting six rupees because of her help in teaching wives of preachers, making a combined salary of sixteen rupees. When he graduated he was appointed to a very difficult field where he worked for a salary of twelve rupees a month. One day he received an offer from Government of forty rupees per month, together with a comfortable home in which to live, in the midst of pleasant surroundings. It came to him as a great temptation, but he and his wife spent the night in prayer and decided that, as God had called them to do spiritual work, they must not be tempted by money. So they remained and worked for several years, living on the twelve rupees a month. This worker has advanced, and is now drawing a salary of seventy rupees a month, while his old classmates, who were not his equals either in intellectual ability or character, are receiving from Government 600 rupees a month."

There are many other evidences showing that everything vital to the success and spread of the Kingdom of Christ depends upon the divine factor. The work of God is not confined to the extraordinary events and experiences of Christian missions. The presence of God cannot be divorced from the usual, from the expected, and be associated only with the so-called miraculous. God's presence and work are also to be seen in the commonplaces of missionary experience and success. For those who are genuine Christians every common bush " is afire with God."

If God's favor and faithfulness are so great, why is it that the success of the missionary enterprise is so limited? Is it not because so many Christians fail to fulfill the conditions required for the forth-putting of divine power? What are these conditions? A mighty, almost irresistible power is conveyed in an ordinary-looking wire cable on two main conditions, proper insulation and perfect contact. If those abroad and at home, who are seeking to make Christ known to all the non-Christian world, can be saved from selfishness, and at the same time preserve their connection with the abounding and never-failing Source of super-human power, they will accomplish what He surely wills—the making of Christ known to all people. Granted a sufficient number of workers with lives dominated by Christ, we may expect that He will put forth mightily His living power. Unless they surrender themselves to Christ and are controlled by His Spirit, unless they work in His power, they had better turn from this service; for unyielding lives and un-spiritual work will only be a hindrance to the enterprise.

It is the Holy Spirit who communicates to Christians the spirit of witness-bearing and evangelization. Wherever His presence and power have been most largely manifested, the limits of the Kingdom are being extended through the personal testimony and preaching of Christian disciples. Not only the clergy but likewise the laity feel the burden of responsibility for making Christ known among their countrymen. They seek to evangelize the outlying and distant regions as

well as their home communities. Every mission field
abounds with illustrations of such activity. A young
Chinese, who was converted when working in the
Malay Peninsula, went to China to study medicine,
and later returned to West Borneo, where as an itin-
erant vendor of Chinese medicines, he traveled far and
wide. Wherever he went he proclaimed the Gospel
with such power that when, at his request, a missionary
was sent from Singapore to examine his work, between
three and four hundred Chinese converts were found
receiving instruction. All these were the direct product of his faithful witness in the midst of great opposition and persecution. The Christians of Korea
and Manchuria are in their evangelistic zeal an example
to the members of the Church in Christian as well as
in other lands. The Rev. J. Goforth bears testimony
that the results of the different evangelistic missions
were just in proportion to the extent the missionaries
and Chinese Christian leaders yielded themselves to
God and sought the power of the Holy Spirit. He
expresses the conviction that " if the Church of Christ
will humble itself under the hand of God, the Holy
Spirit will confirm the preaching of the Word with
unmistakable signs of His presence and power. . . .
I have the strongest of convictions that it would pay
many, many fold for the Church at home and abroad
to cease for a season its busy round of activities and
seek for the Holy Spirit's power as for hidden treas-
ure. Then, as a missionary in Korea said, after the
power of the Spirit came upon the workers at Phyengyang. ' He did more in half a day than all we would

have done in half a year,' or as our preachers and others in Chan-te-fu exclaimed, after the Holy Spirit had swept through the assembly there for ten days with the fires of judgment, ' God has done exceedingly abundantly above all that we asked or thought. In ten days He has done more than we could have done in ten years.' If we would evangelize the world in our day we must get back to the Pentecostal Factor."

The superhuman must be emphasized as never before since the days of the early Church. Christians need a fuller, more constant, and more commanding realization of the personal presence of Christ. Conferences have been held, not infrequently, both on the home field and on the mission fields, at which the problems, methods, and opportunities of the work of world evangelization have received careful consideration, but there has been alarming neglect to face the great central problem, namely, how to translate into actual experience the word of Christ, " He that abideth in me, and I in him, the same beareth much fruit: for apart from me ye can do nothing." Wherever even small groups of Christians have faced this question, and have been responsive to the truth as God has revealed it to them, they have received new accessions of His power, and have then gone forth to achieve triumphs in His name. The new visions, the new plans, the new movements, the new power, will undoubtedly follow when Christ is given His rightful place in His united Church.

Prayer is the method which relates the irresistible might of God to the missionary enterprise. According to the teaching of Christ and the experience of the Church, both in the early centuries and in recent times, the greatest manifestation of divine power is in the pathway of the intercession of His true followers. Every marked advance in the missionary enterprise has been preceded by prayer. Every fresh accession of power which has come upon the workers has been associated with prayer for the Kingdom. Every visitation of the Spirit of God resulting in spiritual awakenings in the home Church and on the mission fields, has been in itself a convincing evidence of the reality of prayer. Behind the wonderful spiritual awakenings in the Telugu country and also in the Tinnevelly District were scores of earnest Christian men and women devoting themselves from day to day to earnest intercession.

Every grave crisis in the expansion of Christianity which has been successfully met, has been met by the faithfulness of Christ's disciples in the secret place. That there is a necessary connection between the prayers of Christians on the one hand, and the revealing of Christ's plan, the raising up of workers, and the releasing of the great spiritual forces of the Kingdom, on the other hand, is a fact as clearly established as any fact can be established. That God has conditioned so largely the extension, the progress, and the fruitfulness of His Kingdom upon the faithfulness and loyalty of His children in prayer, is at the same time one of the deepest mysteries and one of the most wonderful realities.

The Church has not yet discovered, still less begun

to realize, the limitless possibilities of intercession. How to multiply the number of Christians who, with truthful lives, and with clear, unshakable faith in the character and ability of God, will, individually and collectively or corporately as a Church, wield this force for the conversion and transformation of men, for the inauguration and energizing of spiritual movements, and for the breaking down of all that exalts itself against Christ and His purposes—that is the supreme question of foreign missions. From first to last this task, the making of Christ known to all men, is a superhuman work. Every other consideration and plan and emphasis is secondary to that of wielding the forces of prayer. May the Christians throughout the world give themselves as never before to intercession, for this alone will bring to bear upon the sublime work of carrying the Gospel to all the non-Christian world the all-sufficient forces of the Ever-living One, to whom all power is given in heaven and on earth—the Lord Jesus Christ.

POSSIBILITIES OF
THE PRESENT SITUATION

CHAPTER VIII

POSSIBILITIES OF THE PRESENT SITUATION

It is apparent that the situation in the non-Christian world is of such an urgent and critical character as to demand far greater consecration and effort on the part of the Christian Church. It is also clear, that the Church, with the assured manifestation of the power of God, can, by adequate planning, by the creation of a strong home base, and by the development of efficient forces on the mission field, meet the present unique situation. The possibilities of triumphant success resulting from a truly worthy advance by the Church, and the possibilities of grave consequences which would result from a failure to improve the wonderful opportunity, are such as to demand the most serious consideration.

In the first place, there is the possibility of carrying the Gospel to all the non-Christian world. It is possible so far as the accessibility and open-mindedness of the inhabitants of the non-Christian world are concerned. The non-Christian world is known to-day as it never has been before. The work of exploration has been comprehensive, thorough, and, so far as the inhabited parts of the world are concerned, is practically completed. The whole world is remarkably accessible. Improved means of communication have within the past two decades been spread like a network over nearly all the great spaces of the unevangelized world, or are to-day being projected over these regions. For example, railway lines are being rapidly extended in different sections of Africa, in the Levant, in Central Asia, in the Chinese Empire, and in the more populous parts of the East Indies, giving missionaries easy access to hundreds of millions of people who could not have been readily reached even one generation ago.* One of the most significant and hopeful facts with reference to world evangelization is that the vast majority of the people of the non-Christian nations and races are under the sway, either of Christian governments or of those not antagonistic to Christian missions. This should greatly facilitate the carrying out of a comprehensive campaign to make Christ known.

The minds of the people in most countries are more open and favorable to the wise and friendly approach of the Christian missionaries than at any time in the past. In Japan, including Formosa and the Lu-chu Islands, there is almost everywhere a readiness to hear and to consider the Gospel message. The war with Russia opened many doors and made the people much more responsive to the teaching of the Christian religion. The leaders of the nation and other thoughtful men of Japan are feeling the need of a new moral basis, and many of them are looking to Christianity to furnish it. Within a half generation ex-territoriality

* See map at the end of this volume.

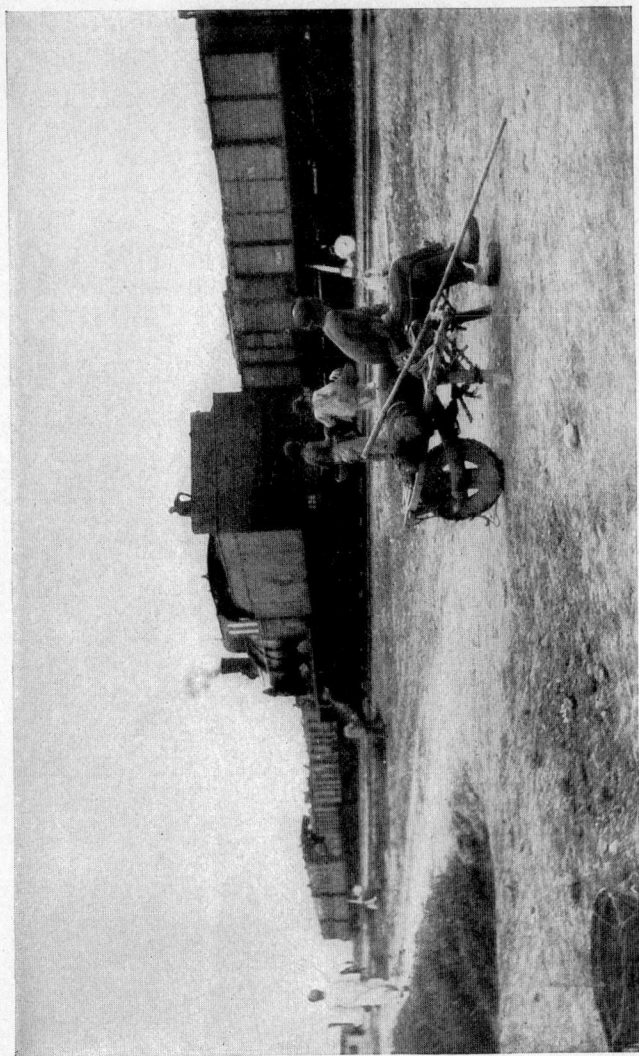

A CHINESE WHEELBARROW AND ITS RIVAL

has been done away with in Japan as a result of the revision of her tre⌐ties with Western nations, thus permitting missionaries to travel, work, and reside in any part of the country.

Almost the whole population of Korea is now ready to listen to the Gospel. The troubles through which these people are passing are causing them to turn in great numbers to Christianity for comfort and strength. Contact with the outside world and the progress of education, as well as the teaching of the missionaries, have swept away many deep-seated superstitions. The authorities are conciliatory, and in some cases directly helpful, to the Christian movement.

It is said that in no part of Manchuria is there open hostility to the Gospel. On the contrary there seems to be marked readiness and willingness to hear and to understand the Christian doctrine. Even in Mongolia the people are more open and responsive to the Gospel appeal than they were a decade ago. In nearly every part of China there are signs that the stolid indifference and the proud aloofness of the past are giving way. Notwithstanding the opposition manifested by some of the officials and other influential men, there is among the people in general a large measure of open-mindedness to what the teachers from the West may have to offer. The native mind seems to be clearer as to the aims and motives of the missionary. This does not necessarily imply that there is a higher valuation put upon Christianity, but it does mean that there is certainly less hostility manifested toward its representatives. This is due chiefly to the removal of ignorance, prejudice and superstition by the dissemination of knowledge, and to the influence of the lives and teaching of the missionaries. A missionary, writing from a province of China which until recently was one of the most exclusive, says that he could not ask for greater friendliness than that with which he now finds among all classes of the people. He expresses the opinion that in no land is there greater liberty for the preaching of the Gospel. One missionary, writing from one of the westernmost provinces of the country, says that, in visiting 224 walled cities where he used to encounter opposition, he now finds none.

A missionary secretary who recently visited all the principal mission fields of Asia has stated that in no other country of Asia except Korea are missionaries regarded with greater friendliness by the people of all ranks than in Siam. Throughout the island of Ceylon the wise missionary can to-day without serious difficulty obtain respectful audiences of non-Christian men for the presentation of the Gospel.

Owing to the great complexity of the situation on the Indian continent it is difficult to express concisely the situation throughout the whole field. By common consent the masses of outcastes and lower castes are more receptive to-day than ever. There is scarcely a limit to the numbers who would place themselves under instruction of properly qualified Christian teachers. Many untutored non-Aryan tribes are awakening to the call of Western civilization and are beginning to listen responsively to the Gospel message.

It is said that the women of India of various castes are coming to have a realizing sense of their needs, and are seeking for education and light. The zenanas are open to a degree which could not have been foreseen a few years ago. Here and there thoughtful, earnest, spiritually-minded Hindus are reading the words of Christ and seeking to understand Him. If Christian intercourse with these important men could now be multiplied, large numbers of them would be led into full and open discipleship.

Workers among Moslems in India all testify that their attitude toward Christ and His people is more friendly and favorable than it was in the last generation. The Parsees, owing to the increase of education and the friendly work of missionaries, are more accessible and responsive than they were a few years ago. The situation in the various native states throughout the Indian peninsula, as well as in the states along the northern border, has improved upon what it was in the last generation. Notwithstanding the many adverse influences and the more pronounced hostility and opposition in certain quarters, it is undoubtedly true that, taking India as a whole, the field is more open than it was twenty, or even ten years ago.

The situation with reference to the spread of the Gospel in Arabia calls for a strong faith and a zeal that knows no discouragement, but the outlook is hopeful, and is growing more so year by year as a result of political developments and of the new railway. Moslems in the Russian Empire are approachable. Great external changes have taken place in the Turkish Empire during the past two years. Even if attention is confined exclusively to the Moslem population, there is satisfactory evidence that work on their behalf, if wisely and prudently conducted, is now possible to a degree which would have been incredible two years ago. Many restrictions have been removed with reference to travel, the holding of meetings, the printing and circulation of literature, and the conduct of schools. Moslems and non-Moslems have been placed upon an equal footing before the law and in the rights of citizenship. This fact alone inaugurates a new era. Mohammedans in these lands have never had an opportunity to understand and accept pure Christianity. Missionaries in different parts of Turkey report a willingness on the part of many Mohammedans to attend Christian gatherings, to talk about Christianity, and to study it in its simplicity and purity. The same thing can be said of the Moslems of Persia. Much is possible there now, provided the work is developed gradually and in a friendly and conciliatory spirit, especially by means of medical and educational missions conducted by wise, spiritual workers.

Throughout the larger part of the vast African continent there is a great and pressing opportunity for the presentation of the claims of Christ. In Mohammedan Africa indeed there is considerable hindrance from government opposition or restrictions. Moslem intolerance has still to be reckoned with among the people, but this intolerance is weakening, and, as the missionaries wisely adapt themselves to the conditions, the way is becoming more and more open. In pagan

Africa not only is the way open, but those to whom the way leads are awaiting the arrival of the messengers. We have been unable to learn of any extensive field throughout the great Island World which is absolutely closed to the wise and devoted ambassador of Jesus Christ.

There are multiplied evidences of larger access and freedom for the proclamation of the Gospel to classes of people in Russia and in many parts of Latin Europe and Latin America who hitherto have been without faith in the living Christ.

When has the Christian Church been confronted with such a wide opportunity as the one now before her in the non-Christian world as a whole? As always, opportunity spells responsibility, and this unparalleled openness comes to the Church as a great test and trial of the reality and the living strength of its faith, and of its capacity for comprehensive Christian statesmanship and generalship.

It is possible to-day as never before to have a campaign adequate to carry the Gospel to all the non-Christian world, so far as the Christian Church is concerned. Its resources are more than adequate. There are tens of millions of communicant members. The money power in the hands of believing Christians of our generation is enormous. There are many strong missionary societies in America, Europe, Australasia, and South Africa, and these have accumulated a vast fund of experience, and have developed a great variety of helpful methods and facilities through several generations of activity throughout the world. Surely they possess directive energy amply sufficient to conceive, plan, and execute a campaign literally worldwide in its scope. The extent, character, and promise of the native Christian Church make it by no means an inefficient part of the Body of Christ.

The abounding energy and tremendous possibilities of the inspiring movements recently called into being will facilitate the realization of the aims of the missionary propaganda: for example, the Student Volunteer Movement; the more comprehensive World's Student Christian Federation; the Young People's Missionary Movement; the Laymen's Missionary Movement; the efficient women's missionary societies; the Foreign Departments of the Young Men's and Young Women's Christian Associations; the various Forward Movements within different Christian communions; the army of youth in the Sunday schools, and various young people's societies and guilds. The Holy Spirit has certainly been preparing and marshaling forces for a campaign commensurate with the missionary responsibility of the Church. Above all there are the superhuman resources: the dynamic power of the Gospel of Christ; the unrealized possibilities of intercession; the triumphant power of holy lives—lives unreservedly yielded to the sway of the risen Christ; and the presence of Christ Himself in His Church by His Spirit, the One Who is able to subdue all things unto Himself. Thus, as followers of Christ look outward over the great areas of the non-Christian world, and then turn to survey the resources of Christendom and to gaze by faith upon their superhuman resources, can they question the possibility to-day of making Christ known to all people?

There is also the possibility of entering now into the heritage of the long period of preparation. Where there have been great causes at work we may expect in due time to witness great results. There is no body of workers in connection with any human enterprise who have devoted themselves to their task with greater intensity, thoroughness, and self-denial than those have shown who have been engaged during the past one hundred years in seeking to carry the Gospel to the non-Christian world. While their numbers have been proportionately small their ability has been of a high order, and their wisdom has been remarkable. This comment applies to a large section of both the foreign and native workers. There is one fact to which far too little importance is attached. Even those missionary efforts which have seemed to yield comparatively small results have not been in vain. While there may not have been many positive results to show from such efforts, yet time will prove that they have been helpful in spreading the Gospel. They have helped to undermine the strength of heathendom. In sections of the Mohammedan and Hindu communities of India, the work of the past one hundred years has been largely that of disintegration, and to-day we see the beginning of the final break-up of these gigantic systems. Were the Christian Church now to advance in the power of Christ, results could be achieved far surpassing anything accomplished in the past.

As Dr. Fulton pointed out at the Centenary Missionary Conference in China, the work of foreign missions has not been unlike that of the work of reclamation carried on in recent years by the United States Government for the purpose of making productive great tracts of desert land. The problem has been that of assuring to those areas streams of water that will bring fertility and fruitfulness—water in steady or regular streams, and not in uncertain quantities or at unknown times. So the work of the missionary enterprise hitherto has been largely that of tunneling mountains and constructing reservoirs and canals so as to be able to convey the water in adequate measure and continuity to the great multitudes in the waste and desert places of the non-Christian world. But this all-important preparatory work has now reached a stage where the life-giving streams should be released in far greater measure.

While the missionaries on every field have tried more or less to secure immediate results, their principal tasks, whether they recognized it or not, have been concerned with the preliminaries of a really adequate advance. Their work has been largely that of scouting and exploring, of organizing and training the arms of the service, of forging the weapons, of evolving the tactics and strategy of the campaign, of sapping and mining, of experimenting. This necessarily prolonged labor is now in many fields complete, and as the Rev. W. H. Findlay, formerly of South India, has pointed out, "The effective advance, with victories eclipsing almost all those of the past, may be con-

fidently expected, if the Church sends the army."
For these preliminary stages the forces thus far employed have not been altogether inadequate. But for
the work now at hand greater numerical strength, as
well as far greater spiritual power, is required.

Three great laws of God, absolutely certain in their
working, have long been in operation throughout the
mission fields; and in the light of Church history it is
reasonable to expect that they have made possible
enormous results. The one thing necessary is for the
Christian Church at the present time to enter into the
heritage so fully prepared by the working of these
unchanging laws. One of these is the law of sowing
and reaping. It has been the unvarying rule of the
Kingdom that where there has been proper sowing, in
due time an abundant harvest may be reaped. Seed
sowing has been going on in nearly all of the mission
fields for a generation, and in many of them for two
or three generations. The seed sown has been good
seed—seed with most highly multiplying vitality. The
sowers have been wise, assiduous, and faithful. The
processes of watering and nurturing have been, generally speaking, efficient. The Lord of the Harvest
has never been found wanting in bringing forth increase. The great thing needed is capable reapers,
abounding in faith and sufficient in number. Granted
such, we shall witness large harvests. Even in the
most difficult fields of the Mohammedan and Hindu
world we shall see the coming out into open confession
of a great company of the now secret disciples of our
Lord. A study of the great harvests in connection

with the progress of Christianity suggests no convincing reason why in many other parts of the non-Christian world, there should not be triumphs and ingatherings like those of recent years in Korea, Manchuria, Northern India, and the East Indies.

Another one of God's laws, equally certain in its operation, is the law of intercession. On the authority of Christ, which is fully supported in the experience of His followers, intercession has limitless achieving power. There is possibly no section of the Christian Church which has devoted itself more fully to real prayer than the leaders of the Christian propaganda in the non-Christian world; and the vital Christians on the home field have probably remembered no other cause in their prayers with greater faithfulness than the movement for the extension of the limits of Christ's Kingdom among the peoples who have not known Him. But of what use is this great and growing volume of intercession unless the Church goes forth in force to enter its rightful possessions? Wherever it has done so with confident apostolic spirit it has invariably been rewarded with abounding success.

The law of sacrifice, like the other two laws which have been named, brings into operation a force adequate to the achievement of vast spiritual results. Christ enunciated the deepest principle underlying the spread of His Kingdom in this language: " Except a grain of wheat fall into the earth and die, it abideth by itself alone; but if it die it beareth much fruit." On this ground may not a wonderful increase be expected in our day? A large number of missionaries and native leaders even within the past two decades, have laid down their lives for the sake of the Kingdom. The whole life and career of the missionary is one of self-denial, in which the members of his family also participate. There has also been a large volume of sacrifice for the missionary cause on the part of many Christians on the home field. But the sacrifices of Christ's followers at home and abroad will have been comparatively fruitless unless the members of the Church, in full recognition of the wonderful possibilities of the working of this law, seek both to harvest the fruits of the sacrifices already made and to associate themselves more fully with Christ in the life of self-sacrifice.

There is the possibility of grave consequences to the Church in Christian lands resulting from its failure to perform its missionary duty. If the Church does not rise to the present situation and meet the present opportunity there will result a hardening of the minds and hearts of its members which will make them unresponsive to God. If the situation now confronting the Church throughout the world does not lead men to larger consecration, and to prompt and aggressive effort, it is difficult to imagine what more God can do to move the Church to perform its missionary duty unless it be to bring upon it some great calamity.

To know the awful need of the non-Christian world, to have available a Gospel abundantly sufficient to meet that need, to be fully able to carry that Gospel to those who are in need of it, and not to do so, will inevitably result in unreality and hypocrisy throughout the home

Church. It is an inexorable law of Christianity that no Christian can keep spiritual life and blessing to himself, but must communicate to those in greatest need. Not to do so damages the character of the Christian himself, promotes like hypocrisy among other Christians who are influenced by him, leads unbelievers around to lose confidence in the reality of Christianity, and leaves in outer darkness multitudes of souls in non-Christian lands, who, were it not for such sham profession, would be ushered into the marvelous light and liberty of Christ. Without doubt the present halting and seeming inaction of the Church is bringing discredit on the name and power of Christianity.

The only thing which will save the Church from the imminent perils of growing luxury and materialism is the putting forth of all its powers on behalf of the world without Christ. Times of material prosperity have ever been the times of greatest danger to Christianity. The Church needs a supreme world-purpose —a gigantic task, something which will call out its energies, something which will throw it back upon God. This desideratum is afforded by the present world-wide missionary opportunity and responsibility. To be able to lay hold in particular of the lives of the strongest young men and young women, the Church must offer them a task of such magnitude as will call forth their heroism. May it not be that God designs that the baffling problem which confronts Christianity in the non-Christian world shall constitute the school for disciplining the faith and strengthening the character

of His followers? To preserve the pure faith of
Christianity, a world-wide plan and conquest are
necessary. This lesson is convincingly taught on the
pages of Church history. The concern of Christians
to-day should not be lest non-Christian people refuse
to receive Christ, but lest they, in failing to communicate Him, will themselves lose Him.

Above all there is the possibility of the enrichment
of the Church. The movement to carry forward an
enterprise to make Christ known to all mankind will
inevitably widen the horizon and sympathies of the
Church. It will be impossible to plan and wage a
world-wide campaign without being enlarged by the
enterprise itself. The life of the Church depends upon
its being missionary. Revivals of missionary devotion
and of spiritual life have ever gone hand in hand. The
missionary activities of the Church are the circulation
of its blood, which would lose its vital power if it
never flowed to the extremities. The missionary problem of the Church to-day is not primarily a financial
problem, but is that of ensuring a vitality equal to the
imperial expansion of the missionary programme.
The only hope of this is for Christians to avail themselves of the more abundant life through Christ be-
stowed in the pathway of obedience to Him.

If God is to manifest mightily His power in the
home Church so that it may be able to grapple successfully with the problems at its own doors, it is essential
that the Church give itself in a larger way to the carrying out of His missionary purposes. Is it not true
that when this main purpose is forgotten or subordin-

ated, a paralysis comes upon the Church, incapacitating it for other efforts? World evangelization is essential to Christian conquest at home. The only faith which will conquer Europe and America is the faith heroic and vigorous enough to subdue the peoples of the non-Christian world.

The apologetic value and influence of a widespread, thorough, and triumphant propagation of the Gospel should also be emphasized. In Christian lands many have lost faith in Christianity as a power to uplift mankind. If the foreign missionary propaganda furnishes from the difficult fields of the non-Christian world evidence showing the ability of the Christian religion to transform men individually, to elevate communities socially, and to win whole nations, the effect on the life and influence of the home Church will be very great indeed. On the other hand, should the missionary enterprise fail to meet successfully the present world-need and opportunity, the faith of many in the mission and power of Christianity may be shaken to the foundation.

Christ emphasized that the mightiest apologetic with which to convince the non-Christian world of His divine character and claims would be the oneness of His disciples. Experience has already shown that by far the most hopeful way of hastening the realization of true and triumphant Christian unity is through the enterprise of carrying the Gospel to the non-Christian world. Who can measure the federative and unifying influence of foreign missions? No problem less colossal and less bafflingly difficult will so reveal to the

Christians of to-day the sinfulness of their divisions, and so convince them of the necessity of concerted effort, as actually to draw them together in answer to the intercessio.. of their common and divine Lord. " It is a gain to the home Church, the importance of which cannot be exaggerated, that, as a result of its foreign mission work, there should be coming back to it from lands not yet Christian powerful influences that are helping to heal its divisions and restore its broken unity."

A programme literally world-wide in its scope is indispensable to enrich and complete the Church. Jesus Christ must have all the races and all the nations through which to make known fully His excellences and to communicate adequately His power. Informed, transformed, enlightened, enlivened by the reception of Christ and the indwelling of the Holy Spirit, Asia, Africa, and Oceania will surely exercise a profound influence upon the Western Church and help greatly to enlarge and enrich its conceptions of Christ and His Kingdom.

The missionary possibilities of the Christian Church to-day are boundless. What limits their realization? There is in the Christ-given missionary purpose of the Church nothing which limits these possibilities, for that purpose is broad enough, in its scope, to embrace the entire non-Christian world and to meet the whole range of needs of each human heart and of the human race. The needs of the non-Christian nations and races present no such limitation; their need is great enough extensively and intensively to require all that Christian lands can give them, and the opportunities they present are sufficiently wide and inspiring to call forth the self-denying devotion of all of Christ's true followers. Nor do the times in which we live suggest a limit to the missionary possibilities of the Church. In no preceding generation or decade has the Church been confronted throughout the non-Christian world with such a coincidence or synchronizing of crises, providences, and favoring conditions. And there is no limit in God as to what He might accomplish, through His children, for the extension of His Kingdom on earth. The only place where such limitations exist is in the lives of Christians. They, by their lack of vision, by their lack of whole-hearted consecration, by their lack of efficient resolution, by their lack of heroic self-sacrifice, and by their lack of triumphant faith, prevent the complete realization of God's sublime purposes for the world. Of how many are the words spoken in olden times still true, " They limited the Holy One." The present is the time of all times when Christians everywhere should rise above all that would hinder the mighty manifestation of Christ in the missionary work of the Church.

It is a decisive hour for the non-Christian nations. Far-reaching movements—national, racial, social, economic, religious—are shaking them to their foundations. These nations are still plastic. Shall they set in Christian or pagan molds? Their ancient faiths, ethical restraints, and social orders are being weakened or abandoned. Shall our sufficient faith fill the void?

It is a decisive hour for the Christian Church. If it neglects to meet successfully the present world crisis by failing to discharge its responsibility to the whole world, it will lose its power both on the home and on the foreign fields and will be seriously hindered in its mission to the coming generation. Nothing less than the adequacy of Christianity as a world religion is on trial.

It is indeed the decisive hour of Christian missions. It is the time of all times for Christians of every name to unite and with quickened loyalty and with reliance upon the living God, to undertake to make Christ known to all men, and to bring His power to bear upon all nations. It is high time to face this duty and with serious purpose to discharge it. Let leaders and members of the Church reflect on the awful seriousness of the fact that times and opportunities pass. The Church must use them or lose them. The sense of immediacy and the spirit of reality are the need of the hour. Doors open and doors shut again. Time presses. " The living, the living he shall praise Thee." Let each Christian so resolve and so act that if a sufficient number of others will do likewise, all men before this generation passes away may have an adequate opportunity to know of Christ.

INDEX

INDEX

PAGE